A STUDY IN CHRISTIAN VOCATION ~ CHRIST AND YOUR JOB

BY ALFRED P. KLAUSLER

"Set your minds, then, on endorsing by your conduct the fact that God has called and chosen you."

(2 Peter 1:10, Phillips)

Concordia Publishing House · Saint Louis, Missouri

41334
May '61

Copyright 1956

Second Printing

Slightly Revised Edition

Copyright 1958 by

Concordia Publishing House
Saint Louis, Missouri

Library of Congress Catalog Card No. 56-9537

Manufactured in the United States of America

CONTENTS

INTRODUCTION

A word of warning to those who are seeking another guide to peace of mind or a manual on job security. This book guarantees neither peace of mind nor job security. Even if you do recognize and appreciate the meaning of Christian vocation, your life will not become automatically free of tensions, problems, heartaches.

No one denies that Christianity alone can make life meaningful here and now. But having the Christian faith doesn't mean that your company might not suddenly fire you or that you will never have a crop failure. As a matter of fact, you, as a Christian, might have an even greater share of troubles than the man next door who thinks Christianity is a lot of tommyrot.

I realize that thoughtful readers might accuse me of advocating Christian activism or a kind of muscular Christianity. This is that type of Christianity, at least so say its defendants, which is only valid through overt acts. You are not a Christian unless you demonstrate your faith.

Thoughtful European churchmen frequently accuse American Christians of being first and last activists.

Perhaps there is some truth in this accusation, for our type of civilization seems to glorify the doer. On the other hand, American Christians have a tendency to look down at the European's preoccupation with theological study.

But don't ever discount the American Christian's activism. I have a tremendous admiration for the American Christian who builds hospitals, clears slums, develops beautiful summer-conference camps, establishes and maintains great colleges and universities, contributes generously to the support of his church. Life in America would be both pointless and completely secular without these manifestations of determined, active Christians — muscular Christians if you will.

There is a danger, however, connected with activism. George W. Forrell has pointed out that many Christians "flee from decision into action. Activity — any activity — becomes the substitute for responsible decision. As a result they confuse the important and the unimportant and lose all opportunity to live a meaningful Christian life. They are so busy everywhere that they cannot even hear what Christ is trying to say to them in His Word." *

Many, many Christians are deeply troubled about this matter of making the Christian faith real in daily living. Having the faith, they want to put it into action and operation. They want to be able to demonstrate the reason for their joy in God's grace. Call this pragmatism or any other peculiar American aberration. The fact is that inherent in the Christian faith there is the impelling force to bring it into everyday living. A divine restless-

---

* George W. Forrell, *Ethics of Decision* (Philadelphia: Muhlenberg Press), p. 40.

ness seizes the Christian. The redeemed individual feels that he cannot be silent as he lives and works.

At the same time he is troubled because he cannot go on a preaching mission while he operates a complicated lathe or a harvesting combine.

The purpose of this book, then, is to offer a study on the Christian vocation and to help clarify the great Scriptural truths about our calling by God through Jesus Christ. It is a study of the meaning of the Christian vocation insofar as our daily lives as Christians are concerned.

In the various chapters I try to point out some of the reasons why we ought to spend time on this great principle and why we ought to saturate ourselves with it. I think it ought to be stressed once more that we live in an age in which so many people seem to have acquired a depressing feeling of futility. This feeling may stem from a variety of social, political, or economic causes. For those who wish a careful and quite challenging study of the nature of our times, I suggest a reading of C. Wright Mills, *The Power Elite,* a disturbing analysis of what makes our society tick.

The Christian frequently succumbs to these feelings of futility if he is not properly grounded in the many aspects of his faith.

There is another startling aspect about contemporary life. There are so many people thoroughly unhappy in their jobs. They regard their daily work merely as a means which provides them with money or other security. Any personnel manager of a corporation will relate almost without prompting the problems he has with discontented employees.

Occasionally, too, I have met Christians who hold

the mistaken notion that the Christian cannot perform God-pleasing work and help the total progress of the Kingdom in his daily occupation. Many devout mothers insist that their sons enter the holy ministry because in this office there is a doubly glorious opportunity to witness dramatically to the faith. This may be true. The holy ministry is a highly blessed calling, but these mothers forget that the Christian employed in the Bureau of Internal Revenue can also render an effective witness to the Christian faith.

And so, because this is an age in which people, both Christians and non-Christians, seek spiritual and material security, it is worth our while to re-examine a Scriptural truth which had a remarkable resurgence in the Reformation and which is now once more the object of earnest study and application throughout the church. I pray that this study in Christian vocation will be a stimulant and a challenge to Christians everywhere. If a non-Christian should happen to read this study, I pray that he will see why the believer in the Lord Jesus Christ is the most blessed of all people.

My indebtedness to William H. Whyte's *The Organization Man* is more than obvious to even the most casual reader. Vance Packard's *The Hidden Persuaders*, which contains a disturbing report on subliminal perception, is a wonderful undergirding for many of the statements in Chapter 1. I also owe a great deal to Martin Mayer's *Madison Avenue, USA*, a penetrating study of American advertising practices and their ultimate effect on both the American and the rest of the world.

Acknowledgment is made to the *Christian Century* for permission to reprint, as part of Chapter 8, my study of the Trumbull Park housing riots; to the *Walther*

8

League Messenger for permission to quote extensively from several articles as indicated in the footnotes; to Concordia Publishing House for the use of part of my pamphlet *The Right Job for You* in Chapter 3. Permission has also been graciously given by the various publishers to use quotations in the body of the text. These quotations are acknowledged in the footnotes.

The dedication is to the memory of my Christian parents, whose love and devotion offered me the first insights into the glories of the Christian vocation.

ALFRED P. KLAUSLER

Chapter 1

THE PREDICAMENT OF MODERN MAN

THE UNHAPPY MAN

IT is one of the ironies of history that the modern American is an unhappy man. This is a generalization that may be attacked at various points. Each one of us knows scores of people who lead happy lives. They are well-adjusted people, happy in their relationships with their families, friends, and associates. They are content with their economic and social status. They are aware of their personal limitations and their particular talents. These are not unhappy people.

On the other hand, it is hard to escape the fact that our modern era has the stigma of an increasing incidence of mental illness. The psychiatrist of our day leads a harried life. His waiting room is filled morning, noon, and night with people who are mentally sick. Careful observers of life in our time have applied to our era such terms as "The Age of Anxiety," "The Era of Frustrations," "The Age of Unbelief," "The Wasteland." The modern poet, novelist, and playwright has seized upon this same theme and exploited it financially. Self-pity therefore seems to be the dominant theme of our time. Are we then, all neurotics, constantly brooding upon our failures and humiliations?

But perhaps there is really nothing wrong with modern man and the modern era. Only the theologians and poets, who are separated from reality anyway, say so, for they must have something to moan about.

There are many vigorous defenders of modern life who say that the large majority of people today are very happy. If modern advertising and the writers of fiction in the pages of the slick magazines are to be believed there is nothing wrong with us. We are all happy people

An observer from another planet studying our advertising would be truly convinced that paradise has at last been achieved in America. Look at the rosy-cheeked children in the modern advertisements. See the happily married couples, the beautiful homes, the tidy bank accounts. There is no problem, whether it is getting someone buried or repairing a scratch on your fender that cannot be solved in a convenient and happy manner Even more wonderful about the world which advertising has created is this, that there are no old people. Only the young populate America. Where there are old people, they are immaculately groomed and financially well-heeled.

The astonished observer, basing his conclusions only on what he sees in the advertising writer's world, would feel that all tears, griefs, and heartaches have been forever abolished. The Garden of Eden is to be found in the glory and splendor that is modern American life.

However, and this is a big "however," the modern American is basically unhappy, insecure, unsure, frustrated. There is ugliness in his life. There is the sordid and the tragic which confronts him either personally or in the immediate world about him. "The nation is full of confused persons who feel that there is something wrong, something deeply unsatisfying about the lives they are living." [1]

This fact can be established. In a survey conducted by the Fund for the Republic in the summer of 1954 it was found that personal problems and family difficulties are of first concern with most people. Fifty per cent of the people interviewed said so.[2]

The most casual reader of the modern newspaper discovers that there are many unhappy people. Many write in daily to the "personal problems" editor.

One could easily find additional proofs of modern man's basic unhappiness.

Coupled with this unhappiness is a phenomenal rise of interest in religion. Church attendance is on the increase, and church membership has reached the amazing total of 100,000,000. Books on religion enjoy an astonishing vogue. It has become popular to go to church and to be interested in religion.

All this is one indication, some think, of man's search for an escape. Grateful as churchmen are over this amazing interest, they nevertheless wonder whether this is an interest revolving primarily around self-interest and self-preservation.

The late Paul Hutchinson, a keen observer of the religious trends of the times, said that people need the

---

[1] *Life,* April 11, 1955.

[2] Samuel A. Stouffer, *Communism, Conformity, and Civil Liberties* (Doubleday, 1955).

reassurance of religion so much that the quest of such assurance has become a cult, as exemplified by the popularity of Dr. Norman Vincent Peale.

In the following three sections I shall point out three areas of disturbance which should jar us out of our complacency. They indicate that the predicament in which modern man finds himself is almost without parallel in history.

THE ABSENCE OF GOD

Despite the apparent revival of interest in religion, it seems to be almost axiomatic to say that God continues to be dethroned in almost all areas of life. Though civic, political, and educational leaders generally pay public tribute to God, they frequently show by their actions that they haven't any concept of faith in God and regard for His Law. The ancient moral heresy of the end justifying the means is to be found not only in Moscow but also in the U. S. Senate, as witness one Senator's insistence that it is absolutely necessary to kick an opponent below the belt to score a point. The applause greeting this statement was almost deafening.

This dethronement of God, this form of unbelief, creates unhappiness in the lives of people and is the great sin of our time. Viewing this situation from another angle, we may say that the great sin of our age is not only this, that God is excluded from all thinking and doing, but also this, that *man* is now the central object in all thinking. An acute British thinker writes: "Men's minds are obsessed with Man. There is the root sin of Western civilization. It is the enthronement of Man at the center of life, being, and thought. . . . It is the great sin, the titanic, Promethean sin. It is the sin of believing

14

and behaving as though Man were an end in himself; as though humanity existed in its own right and for the sole purpose of its glory and power." [3]

This deification of man has had a variety of observable consequences.

The virtual abolition of other-worldliness is now a fact. Man's life on this planet is all the life there is for him. The grave ends the agony. This point of view perhaps explains the Oxford undergraduate's calm, fatalistic contemplation of the A-bomb: "At last, we feel, there is something truly final, something we can't be expected to do anything about. And since no one will ask our permission before using it, we can regard it with the polite calm with which we can contemplate death in general: one doesn't expect to avoid it indefinitely and can't decently complain when it catches up with one." [4]

Because man has been placed in a central position, the things of the spirit have in too many instances vanished or been pushed back into the periphery. In the field of arts, for example, it is highly important that a book must sell, a play must attract large audiences, a motion picture must be filmed with the box office kept firmly in mind. Not too long ago, the New York *Times* reported an advertising executive expressing concern that television plays or productions might become too good, thus detracting from the advertiser. Material matters must of necessity dominate because unregenerate man

---

[3] D. R. Davies, *The Sin of Our Age* (Macmillan, 1947), pp. 23 and 33.

[4] *Time*, December 27, 1954.

is a child of fallen Adam and appreciates only that which is material and tangible.

Another result of this deification of man in our time is the paradoxical situation of man's degradation. As among the beasts, the strong oppress the weak. His individuality is lost in the massman. Since the strong man is now God and it is a fact that man can be manipulated, man can also be subjected to bestial methods; for man is a beast. This is most strikingly illustrated in the development of the brainwashing techniques used by the Communists. The concentration camps of North Korea are simply an extension of the deification and degradation of man. Here in these camps man is regarded as a type of automaton controlled by a series of conditioned reflexes which may be changed at the whim of the leader.

Nor are the Communists the only ones who fall into this error of regarding man as a unit to be manipulated. Some American corporations deliberately cultivate techniques by which both management and workers are molded to the thinking which follows a corporation line. For those interested in the developments in this area a reading of David Riesman's brilliant *The Lonely Crowd* will show how the massman can be controlled and directed by the clever public-relations man. In fact, some of the group-work techniques in use today are used also by corporations to obtain *Gleichschaltung* among their workers.

"A world in which man elbows God out of the position of centrality is necessarily a world which must become self-sufficient, supreme, and exclusive." [5] Nothing is more hated by the believer in dialectic materialism

---

[5] Davies, loc. cit.

or Marxist Communism than the belief in another world and in God as the Ruler of the universe; for such a belief makes man dependent on an outside agent who can never be controlled.

We meet, however, not only the openly expressed, but also the implied deification of man, and, astonishingly enough, in the church. Many professed Christians have become infected by heresies of various kinds, not the least of which is Pelagianism, that ancient heresy of the fifth century. This heresy contends that man has certain inherent moral powers which unaided can effect his conversion and salvation. Man is given powers which belong only to God.

The living and thinking of the average man today has been complicated by the development of the A-bomb and the H-bomb. Today man must make a choice between unprecedented material progress which nuclear fission can bring him and widespread death and devastation.

Thomas E. Murray, commissioner of the United States Atomic Energy Commission, startled his audience by saying: "I consider it no exaggeration, but the sober truth, to say that atomic energy has resulted in the greatest change in man's relations with nature since the fateful day in the Garden of Eden." All the more now man likes to think of himself as a god, who has power over life and death.

And yet man sees that his self-deification is self-deception. Since he is emotionally inclined to that which is brutal and horrible and since man almost instinctively knows that any weapons developed will be used for man's destruction, it is not surprising that air-raid drills, the placing of Nike stations, and Air Force bases on the

17

constant ready, place the average man in a less than peaceful state of mind. Many are inclined to curse science which has brought man to such a predicament. Man has seized an angry bear by the tail and now finds he cannot let loose. Arthur Guiterman somewhat facetiously sums up these developments in this bit of characteristic versifying, entitled "The March of Science":

> First, dentistry was painless;
> Then bicycles were chainless,
> And carriages were horseless,
> And many laws enforceless.
>
> Next, cookery was fireless,
> Telegraphy was wireless,
> Cigars were nicotineless,
> And coffee caffeinless.
>
> Soon oranges were seedless,
> The putting green was weedless,
> The college boy was hatless,
> The proper diet fatless.
>
> Now motor roads are dustless,
> The latest steel is rustless,
> Our tennis courts are sodless,
> Our new religions godless.[6]

PUBLIC LIFE

The uncertainties in modern political life contribute to bewilderment in the modern man and at the same time add to his perplexities and feeling of being trapped in a predicament for which he has no solution. What is decided today in Washington, Peiping, Moscow, Bandung, or Capetown affects everyone within a short period of time.

---

[6] *Gaily the Troubadour* (E. P. Dutton).

Diplomats and politicians scurry from one capital to another and from one conference chamber to the next in an endless quest for peace or for a calm community life, but the net result of all this scurrying frequently is only more confusion, and the average man becomes quite cynical.

The disclosures of secret meetings at which the fate of the world is decided by a group of men whose religious faith is either nonexistent or rather superficial is another contributing factor to the general feeling of insecurity.

It is no wonder that men regard people in government with suspicion. When politicians and statesmen claim they are churchmen and make open profession of their faith and at the same time lend themselves to dubious schemes, one begins to wonder. It is not surprising, then, to note the despair in the hearts of many men. In his penetrating book *Moral Man and Immoral Society* Reinhold Niebuhr points out that men are caught in an impersonally immoral society; and when they attempt to adjust their own good intentions to modern conditions, they see they are met only with failure. And so they despair.

No wonder, therefore, that modern man in this predicament feels that his religion and personal faith is something which is best kept completely separate from the maddening confusion of our time. Who would dare bring his Christian faith into play in Chicago ward politics or in the redistricting of voting areas in the state of Illinois? He would only be laughed at for being a "do-gooder" or derided for seeking the publicity which comes from being a church member.

And yet the need is there. One high government official has stated: "We particularly need spiritual leaders, a handful of men and women who live at the height of the Christian Gospel in all its concrete fullness. They are needed as the leaven in the mass, as lights amid the darkness, as strong cities set upon hills." [7]

THROW SOMETHING AWAY!

If there is this confusion in the hearts of men because of the way politics is carried on, what shall one say about the depersonalization of the individual, the development of "automation," and the use of various psychological techniques by modern corporations to utilize individual capacities to the fullest extent? It is almost unnecessary to comment on the ruthlessness of executive procedures which squeeze a man dry of all his creative ingenuity and then toss him to one side. A recent movie, *Executive Suite*, portrays with cold clarity how men are governed in the modern business and corporation world.

The world we live in is a society that is scientific, technological, industrial, and administrative. This does not mean that the majority of people are engaged in industrial or technical pursuits, but the fact is that the industrial outlook still governs man's general outlook.

J. H. Oldham has brilliantly analyzed modern industrial pursuits by stating that they are governed by functional rationality. This is a technical way of saying that all actions are organized to reach a previously defined goal. The production of goods is the be-all and end-all of modern industry. In fact, someone has said that the "Gospel of Production" is the one gospel understood by modern man. Thus in the drive for lower costs and greater output per man-hour all the technical skills

---

[7] Thomas Murray, U. S. A. E. C., November 8, 1954.

of industrial engineering and production planning are enlisted. The demands of the competitive market require new methods, new ideas, the most economical use of capital and labor.

It is for this reason that automation is on the increase, with machines which practically live and breathe and which seem even to think. Because mass production is so necessary, more machines are required. Men get tired; machines don't. The machines set the pace. It has been estimated that it requires a unit of three men to keep up with one unit of the machine. The person has become an anonymous, interchangeable unit. Work loses its personal quality. A recent series of articles in the Chicago *Sun-Times* presented interviews with workers on the assembly line. They were asked what they thought of their jobs and whether they actually enjoyed them. It was significant that most workers said they liked their jobs because they didn't have to think about what they were doing. They could think about their garden plot or what they would do when they retired.[8]

Since many workers are reduced to such a depersonalized status, it is not surprising they cannot see the social significance of their jobs. The worker in a factory fails to see his responsibility to the community as a whole. How can he see that his work contributes to the good of the community?

This does not say that management and the corporation are not attempting to solve these and similar problems. Personnel workers in factories, even industrial chaplains, are part of the factory scene. Through com-

[8] J. B. Oldham, *Work in Modern Society* (Morehouse-Goreham, 1950), a brilliant analysis of modern technological and industrial developments.

pany publications, movies, and group social activities, the workers are made to feel that they are important parts of a whole and that their contribution is a valued addition to modern society.

In Cameron Hawley's novel *Executive Suite*, one of the characters says: "No man can work for money alone. It isn't enough. You starve his soul when you try it — and you starve a company to death in the same way."

Elton Mayo in *Social Problems of an Industrial Civilization* made a study of large factories. Dr. Mayo states that management "has come to the absurdly simple conclusion that every worker likes to feel his work important." [9]

Though the gospel of production is holding full sway today, one ought not to decry all its benefits. Material well-being is a blessing which few people in past ages ever heard about or even had the remotest idea of. Full employment seems to be the accepted norm in our time. The stock market, as a reflection of current trends, certainly shows that we have never had it so good before. The average income is higher than ever before, and more people are able to buy the necessities as well as the small and large luxuries. A car or a television set is no longer regarded as a luxury. Presumably the time is not too distant when mink coats will be necessities, provided the mink can be sold on the gospel of production.

And yet with this growth in material well-being there has not been a corresponding growth in happiness. It is a truism that while we never had it so good before, there is more unhappiness today. The lines form to

---

[9] *Social Problems of an Industrial Civilization* (Routledge and K. Paul, 1949).

22

the right outside the psychiatrists' clinics. Alcoholism, juvenile disturbances, disciplinary problems, neuroticism, psychic disorders, the grosser crimes, and divorce — these are also present on the current scene. Man presumably cannot solve his own difficulties even though his material well-being is assured. More and more people are covered by social security or other types of insurance. So there is no worry about old age.

And after old age? There is death. But death today is beautified. It is vulgar to mention the grave and death, decay and corpse.

> Death on the American Plan is practiced in a temple of make-believe known as the Funeral Home. The shrine is constructed, as often as possible, along the lines of a country club and rectory combined. Outside, there are gracious plantings of evergreens — designed to "create favorable public sentiment." Inside, there is a sumptuous succession of music rooms, chapels, lavatories, storerooms, and, of course, "slumber rooms." The decoration is "subdued but cheerful," which enables many funeral homes, when their business is lagging, to rent space to wedding parties. And here, where the reek of euphemism mingles with the chemical deodorant and the recorded hymn, has been perfected "the new aesthetic of death," a specifically American response to the handwriting on the wall.[10]

We even have the striking paradox in our time of an overabundance of material goods. There are surpluses of farm products. Car dealers groan over having to dispose of a large quota every week. Appliance dealers have similar difficulties. How to handle this overproduction creates difficulties in many areas. It is baffling the executives of our time.

---

[10] *Time*, October 24, 1955.

In the silver industry the economics of mass production get all snarled up at this point. The greatest boon the industry could have would be a lot of customers who junked their sterling from time to time or periodically turned it in on a new pattern. But being well-nigh imperishable, silver is never junked. And most women tend to think of their sterling as a sentimental treasure, which makes any suggestion of trading it in sound somehow unfaithful. As a result, the manufacturers frequently think of themselves as being hoist on their own drop presses.

John D. Shaw, an executive of International Silver, tells a story on himself that shows how it feels to be up there. In his own kitchen one night a dinner fork fell into the garbage grinder and got badly chewed up. Fishing it out, his wife dried it and tenderly laid it back in the silver drawer.

"No," said Shaw, "throw it away." When she made no move to do so, he reached for the fork, bent it into an approximate likeness of a pretzel, and dropped it into the dust bin. Unaccountably to his wife, he seemed quite worked up. "In this country," he shouted, "somebody, somewhere, sometime or other, has got to throw something away!" [11]

It is for this reason that modern advertising, according to Joseph Wood Krutch, encourages emphasis on "psychological obsolescence rather than the physical wearing out of products" and on "working hard to buy things you don't need and thereby keep other people working hard to make them." A Baltimore advertising man, in replying to this criticism, plaintively asked the

---

[11] *Saturday Evening Post*, April 16, 1955, p. 92.

question, "Why should people buy what is good for them instead of what they want?" An Ohio advertising executive said we should place increasing emphasis on psychological obsolescence because "the expansive industrial capacity of our nation won't operate on the frugal philosophy of 'make it do.' " [12]

As the thoughtful Christian surveys the world around him and sees the predicament of modern man, a predicament in which he is frequently involved, he wonders and ponders. Does the church have an answer? Is there a specific to be found in Holy Scripture? Is the Christian faith relevant to these many modern problems? Can one turn confidently to the Gospel and find a solution which will bring some order out of the chaos in contemporary life? How can the Christian achieve at least a modicum of peace of mind? Is there some way to recognize the fact of sin and the role of Jesus Christ in modern living? Or must a Christian be a thoroughgoing pessimist and accept a *status quo* existence until we have left this vale of tears for the realms of glory? If it is true that "Christianity, in the most profound sense, is a religion for failures," must we, then, assume that nothing can be done with our faith for life in this world?

The church does have an answer, an answer which is outlined in Holy Scripture in a most specific sense. If the concept of the Christian vocation is studied, appreciated, and then applied, much of the tragic confusion of our time can be understood, and the glory of the Christian life can be a reality in all our lives.

---

[12] *Time,* May 22, 1955, p. 28. See also A. C. Spectorsky's *The Exurbanites* (J. B. Lippincott, 1955), a devastating study of the "symbol manipulators," that peculiar American breed which sets the styles and dreams the dreams of the rest of America.

Chapter 2

DEFINING VOCATION

THE word *vocation* occurs only once in the King James translation of Holy Scripture. "I, therefore, the prisoner of the Lord, beseech you that ye walk worthy of the vocation wherewith ye are called" (Eph. 4:1). Goodspeed translates the passage thus: "So I, the prisoner for the Lord's sake, appeal to you to live lives worthy of the summons you have received." J. B. Phillips paraphrases the verse: "As God's prisoner, then, I beg you to live lives worthy of your high calling." The Revised Standard Version renders the passage thus: "I therefore, a prisoner for the Lord, beg you to lead a life worthy of the high calling to which you have been called."

Although the word *vocation* occurs only here, nevertheless synonyms of it occur rather frequently. The concept *vocation,* or *call,* is found throughout Holy Scripture. It is a word which is an integral part of the relationship between God and man. In Genesis we have the remarkable instance of God calling Abraham into an intimate, highly personal, and responsible relationship.

26

"Now the Lord had said unto Abram, Get thee out of thy country, and from thy kindred, and from thy father's house, unto a land that I will show thee" (Gen. 12:1). One commentator points out that Abraham became not a mere wanderer but a pilgrim, because God had called him to a particular task in life. He was to be the progenitor of that race from which the Messiah should be born. The writer to the Hebrews says of him: "By faith Abraham, when he was called to go out into a place which he should receive for an inheritance, obeyed; and he went out, not knowing whither he went" (Heb. 11:8).

We note that here in the Old Testament, at the beginning of time, so to speak, a call from God implied also that faith was involved, that a man hearing this call believed that God was with him and that His promises were sure. This same commentator remarks that, properly understood, the entire Old Testament is the Book of the Vocation of Israel, the "chosen people" of God.[1]

Now, the word *vocation* as used in Holy Scripture and this essay has a variety of meanings.

Vocation may be —

1. The action on the part of God of calling persons or mankind into a state of salvation or union with Himself; the fact or condition of being so called.

2. The action on the part of God in calling a person to exercise some special function, especially of a spiritual nature; or to fill a special position; divine influence or guidance toward a definite, especially religious, career; the fact of being called or directed toward a special work in life; natural tendency to, or fitness for, such work.

---

[1] W. R. Forrester, *Christian Vocation* (Scribner's), p. 24.

3. The particular function or station to which a person is called of God; a mode of life or sphere of action regarded as so determined.[2]

Within the past years the word *vocation* has undergone many changes. Today it is mainly regarded as referring to the job you have in life. We think of it in relation to the career we choose for life. Hence we have the development of such word combinations as "vocational guidance."

This is a pity because, properly understood, the word is a beautiful word, one which helps us realize the presence of God in our lives and one which establishes the intimate relationship between us and our Lord. Emil Brunner says: "It is a conception which in its Scriptural sense is so full of force and so pregnant in meaning, it gathers up so clearly the final meaning of God's acts of grace — the Calling — and the concrete character of the Divine Command in view of the world in which man has to act, that to renounce this expression would mean losing a central part of the Christian message. We must not throw it away, but we must regain its original meaning."[3]

Before delving deeper into the theology or the Scriptural teachings of the Christian vocation, we shall find it worth our time to consider the historical development of the concept of vocation.

It is significant that in the New Testament there is no reference to the idea many people hold that one

---

[2] W. R. Forrester, *Christian Vocation* (Scribner's). Adapted from *A New English Dictionary on Historical Principles.*

[3] W. R. Forrester, quoting Emil Brunner, *The Divine Imperative,* pp. 205, 206.

calling is higher than another. It is also significant that the derogatory references to a calling originate with the critics of the Gospel. One enlightening passage is Matthew 13:55, where the question is asked: "Is not this the carpenter's son?" The reference occurs after Jesus had told a series of parables and had explained the kingdom of God to the people. The view which prompts the question is that of a snob. How can a carpenter's son, one who has no social standing or religious training, presume to offer learned or profound comment on sacred things? A carpenter's calling was not the type to lend itself to studiousness. The question does not imply that being a carpenter is a degrading calling, but indicates that it is inferior to the one in which Jesus is active.

Nowhere do we find that Jesus ever made a slighting reference to any occupation. Nor did St. Paul, apostle though he was, ever feel he was demeaning himself because he was obliged to associate with fishermen, soldiers, tax collectors, or because temporarily he engaged in his trade of tentmaking.

Luther made this significant statement in regard to the Virgin Mary:

Behold, how completely Mary traces all to God, lays claim to no works, no honor, no fame. She conducts herself as before, when as yet she had naught of all this; she demands no higher honors than before. She is not puffed up, does not vaunt herself, nor proclaim with a loud voice that she is to become the Mother of God. She seeks not any glory, but goes about her wonted household duties, milking the cows, cooking the meals, washing pots and kettles, sweeping out the rooms, and performing the work of maidservant or housemother in lowly and despised tasks as though she cared naught for such exceeding great gifts and graces. She was esteemed among other women and her neighbors no more highly than before, nor desired to be, but remained a poor townswoman, one of the great multitude.

When men accord us praise and honor, we ought to profit by the example of the Mother of God. . . . We ought neither to reject this praise and honor as though they were wrong nor to despise them as though they were naught; but . . . ascribe them to Him in heaven to whom they belong.[4]

In short, one may readily assume that all callings were regarded as honorable in the New Testament. There were no gradations in rank. A soldier was not considered as holding a higher position than a housewife; nor was a slave different from a tax collector. All callings were considered within their framework as opportunities to glorify God. Says St. Paul: "So ordain I in all churches. . . . Let every man abide in the same calling wherein he was called."

YOU ARE INFERIOR

What brought about the change in the ranking of callings? Why did the calling of service in the church assume a higher status while those who were tradesmen or artisans were considered to be lesser creatures? The exact point in history when this change-over occurred is hard to determine. Perhaps the rise of the doctrinal disputes centering in the heresies of the church of the early centuries may have helped in the development of a feeling that there was a need for specialists able to handle the heretics. The layman, not having the time to devote to lengthy study and disputation, preferred to let the clergy of the church battle untruth. There was

---

[4] "Commentary on the Magnificat." Quoted in *A Treasury of the Kingdom,* compiled by E. A. Blackburn (Oxford, 1954).

a need for a professional class thoroughly conversant with philosophy, linguistics, theology. It would be almost natural, because of their success in combating these heresies, that the clergy should be considered superior in rank. Their ability to save the church made them marked or different men.

Others feel that Emperor Constantine's official recognition of the church, after centuries of persecution, granted special status to the clergy since they were the leaders of the congregations. The bishops had a close relationship with the government. Human nature being what it is and government always arrogating rights or privileges to itself, it seemed natural to assume that a clergyman was invested with superior authority.

The rise of the various monastic orders, preceded by the increasing number of men and women choosing the ascetic life, contributed to the feeling that these people were indeed obtaining, as the church taught they were, special favor or merit by leading a life which denied the demands of the flesh. People naturally felt that these ascetics, through the admiration they excited among their contemporaries, had attained a special rank before God, aside from the explicit teaching of the church that their calling was truly a sacred one, far superior, for instance, to a humble hotel porter's.

As the monastic orders developed in Europe, the monasteries were one of the few places where learning was fostered. Within the walls of these monasteries the skills, arts, and crafts were nurtured. Here again the inhabitants of these monasteries acquired special status. Along with this, of course, was the evolvement of the teaching that the priest, officiating before the altar, was the intermediary between man and God. With his hands and through his efforts he approached the throne. He alone could grant forgiveness and dispensation to the sinner.

The impact of the Crusades, besides being a cultural one, also helped create special position for those who participated in the Crusades to the Holy Land. He who was able to bear arms against the infidel and free the sacred places in the land of the Savior was given special sanction. Those not able to enroll in a Crusade felt they occupied an inferior position. No matter what their status in life, they did not have the rank of a Crusader.

By the time the Middle Ages were in full swing the average man's role in life was decidedly inferior. No matter whether he was a banker, a laborer, or a peasant, he could not appear on an equal footing. Most to be pitied were the peasants. Their class simply had no status. No matter how faithfully they attended mass and no matter how much they contributed to the support of the church, they were inferior people. Remember that at this time Europe was considered Christian. All were members of the one church, the Holy Roman Church. The Holy Roman Empire gathered all into her domain.

This 13th-century peasant lived a miserable life, even though he was in the church, even though he was baptized. Here is a description by a 13th-century writer, Gautier de Coincy, of the status of the peasant:

> They are ever an unquiet crew, laborious and unclean. They bring to the nearest town whatsoever each has gained either from his field or from the produce of his flock; and here they buy in return whatsoever each needeth; for they have few or no artificers dwelling

32

among them. On holy days they come all together in the morning to the church, whereof there is commonly one for each village; there they hear from their priest God's Word and the sacrament *(sacra);* then, after noon, they treat of their own affairs under a linden tree or in some other public place. After this, the younger folks dance to the sound of the pipe, while the older go to the tavern and drink wine. No one goeth unarmed in public; each has his sword by his side for any chance emergency. [5]

The church was to blame for this sad state, in which classes were ground down, for the church was supreme at that time. The church had a monopoly on life. All children were baptized into the church, and where parents omitted this sacrament, heresy was presumed.

This stricture is not to deny that the church helped preserve some of the cultural heritage of past ages, but this preservation does not compensate for the oppression of classes, the establishment of a hierarchy of values, the rise of corruption in the church, largely due to the conceit of the clergy that they, and they alone, had the right to determine who was to go to heaven.

By the time of the Reformation, discontent was rife among many people and many classes. It was obvious that a foul and cancerous growth was eating away at all that men held most precious. The clergy were arrogant. Illiteracy was the accepted order of the day. Education was granted only to those who were of a certain social position or who were determined, come what may, to have their children rise above their present miserable status.

---

[5] Quoted in *Ethics in a Business Society,* by Marquis Childs and Douglass Cater (Mentor Library), p. 20.

Under these conditions it is no wonder that the Reformation made such a shattering impact on men and events of that time and of generations to come. For the result of Martin Luther's rediscovery of Holy Scripture and his determination to make the Word of God relevant once more in the lives of men was to revolutionize both the church and society; it was to give man new status both before God and man.

What is Martin Luther's great contribution to the world? It is, of course, his rediscovery of the doctrine of justification by faith. Now, it can be demonstrated that once the doctrine of justification by faith is accepted, all else follows. The only difficulty with such a demonstration is that with time man will forget the intermediary steps and sometimes even the final answer. Like every mathematical problem, it must be demonstrated to understand the solution.

Let it forever be remembered, there was once a time when man was perfect. He lived in a glorious relation with God. They were friends. They lived in intimate companionship. It was a perfect relationship, unmarred by misunderstanding or envy. Then man listened to the blandishments of God's archenemy, Satan, and practically within a moment this perfect relationship was destroyed. Man desired to have equal status with God, even though the achievement of that status depended on the violation of God's law. Man fell and was expelled from Paradise, but God graciously gave him the great promise of a Redeemer to come, by faith in whom hope was kept alive in the hearts of all believers. There came in the reign of Caesar Augustus the glorious day when the inexplicable, the wonderful, happened.

There is born in an obscure Judean village a Man of a humble mother. He spends His childhood, adolescence, and young manhood in a Galilean village, under the tutelage of His foster father. During those quiet years this young Man attends the village synagog school and learns His father's trade.

Soon this private life becomes a public career, and all men have the opportunity to see that here at last is the Mediator promised by God since the Fall. This Jesus of Nazareth wanders about the countryside, talking to people, gathering followers, performing miracles, speaking sharply about the corruption present in the church. He announces Himself as the Savior.

He is accused of fomenting rebellion, of uttering blasphemy, of disturbing the *status quo*. On a series of charges He is haled before the courts of the land and is sentenced to die. He is crucified between two robbers. He dies and is buried. He does not remain buried. On the third day He rises again and lives here in this world another forty days before He ascends into heaven.

What we say, therefore, is that for a certain period in time the divine-human Redeemer lived visibly in this world. Had you and I lived then, we might have reached out our hands and touched — GOD! It is a profound mystery, for through the life, death, and resurrection of Jesus Christ, all men, by believing on Him, may reestablish that relationship which had been shattered centuries ago in the Garden of Eden. St. Paul epitomizes it thus: "They [the sinners] are justified by His grace as a gift, through the redemption which is in Christ

35

Jesus, whom God put forward as an expiation by His blood, to be received by faith" (Rom. 3:24, 25, RSV).

Martin Luther once said: "When I am told that God became man, I can follow the idea, but I just do not understand what it means. For what man, if left to his natural promptings, if he were God, would humble himself to lie in the feed box of a donkey or to hang upon a cross? God laid upon Christ the iniquities of us all.

"This is that ineffable and infinite mercy of God which the slender capacity of man's heart cannot comprehend and much less utter — that unfathomable depth and burning zeal of God's love toward us. And truly the magnitude of God's mercy engenders in us not only a hardness to believe but also incredulity itself. For I hear not only that the omnipotent God, the Creator and Maker of all things, is good and merciful but also that the Supreme Majesty was so concerned for me, a lost sinner, a son of wrath and of everlasting death, that He spared not His own Son but delivered Him to the most ignominious death, that, hanging between two thieves, He might be made a curse and sin for me, a cursed sinner, that I might be made just, blessed, a son and heir of God. Who can sufficiently declare this exceeding great goodness of God?" [6]

Therefore we dare never regard the death and resurrection of Jesus Christ as simply a historical phenomenon. These historical facts involve everyone personally. The unbeliever is involved just as surely as the believer. The unbeliever, if he denies the relevance of this fact to his own life, loses his life eternally; the Christian, if he

---

[6] Quoted by Roland H. Bainton in *Here I Stand*, p. 223.

regards this blameless life and this vicarious atonement as accomplished for him, knows that he, too, is involved.

So all Christians stand before God pleading the life and work of Christ Jesus as their own; for He became the Burden-Bearer. It is only through Him that God may be approached. "I am the Door," John 10:7; "I am the Way," John 14:6. "He is the only Bridge on which man can cross the abyss of sin that separates him from God. He is the Foundation that alone supports our tottering existence." [7] Man has not been and never will be able to earn the forgiveness which is his through faith in Christ. Try as he might to achieve peace with God through his efforts, he cannot. "To you Christ has given life! . . . Even though we were dead in our sins, God was so rich in mercy that He gave us the very life of Christ (for it is, remember, by grace and not by achievement that you are saved) and has lifted us out of the old life to take our place with Him in Christ in the heavens." (Eph. 2:4.)

Thus it is that because God has extended this unmerited mercy to us, we are called by Him. We belong to the category of the called of God. We belong to a glorious fellowship. You are God's "chosen generation," His "royal priesthood," His "holy nation," His "peculiar people" — all the old titles of God's people now belong to the Christian. We are the chosen generation. The Sacrament of Holy Baptism is the initial act which stamps for all time that we are now God's. Through this faith we are made holy. "He saved us — not by virtue of any moral achievements of ours, but by the

---

[7] Adolf Koeberle, *The Quest for Holiness* (Augsburg), p. 54.

cleansing power of a new birth and the moral renewal of the Holy Spirit, which He gave us so generously through Jesus Christ, our Savior" (Titus 3:5).

FORGIVENESS

As a result, we say, first of all, God called us out of darkness — the darkness of our inner and outer corruption resulting from our fellowship with Satan — into the marvelous light of His love in Christ, our Savior. Once we have been called into membership with this fellowship, we discover furthermore that we must still live in this world and that we are required, as the children of God, to live in a world basically hostile to the things of God. None the less the requirement is laid on us that we must live both in the world as the children of God and in the fellowship of saints as the called of God.

Our life is, therefore, lived constantly in the aura of the forgiveness of sins. The motivation for living a sanctified life comes first from the Holy Spirit. "I believe that the Holy Spirit has called me by the Gospel, enlightened me with His gifts, sanctified and kept me in the true faith."

Although mere acceptance of the fact that God has forgiven us our sins is sufficient for salvation, we must for various reasons acknowledge the obligations laid on us by our faith in the words of St. James, "Faith without works is dead." But we must be on our guard lest we place faith in a secondary position. Luther points out in his tract *The Freedom of the Christian Man:* "Faith is enough for the Christian man. He has no need for works to be made just. Then he is free from the Law. But he is not therefore to be lazy or loose. Good works do not make a man good, but a good man does good

38

works." [8] "As there is no need to tell lovers what to do and say, so is there no need for any rules to those who are in love with Christ." [9]

This love of the Gospel and this living of the forgiveness of sins can be found in a monastery or in any specific secular calling. The Gospel can be exemplified anywhere. The priesthood belongs to all believers. We may approach the altar.

YOU ARE FREE, AND YOU ARE A SINNER

"Since we are in the world but not of the world, we must work. God has placed us here. God no longer walks upon this earth. He works through His creatures whom He has placed here. Our works are God's masks, behind which he does all things." [10]

The Bible is filled with references to work. In fact, the very first verse of the Bible speaks of work. God worked when He created the heavens and the earth. If we may speak in human terminology, it was God's calling to work as a Creator, just as it was Adam and Eve's calling to work in the Garden of Eden.

As we have been called to be the children of the Lord Jesus, we also have our duties in life. We have a place in the world. "Live lives worthy of your high calling. Accept life with humility and patience, making allowance for each other because you love each other. . . . Naturally there are different gifts and functions; individually, grace is given to us in different ways out of the

---

[8] Bainton, p. 230.

[9] Bainton, p. 230.

[10] Luther, *Day by Day We Magnify Thee*, trans. Steiner and Scott, p. 299.

rich diversity of Christ's giving." And in the remaining verses of Ephesians 4, as well as in other chapters, St. Paul points out how we have been called and how we are to live. Since he gives instruction on how to live in various callings, God must want His Christians to serve in them. Also St. Peter points out that our life is to be worthy of our high calling (1 Peter 2:11—4:11).

In a sermon preached in 1531 Luther said: "Therefore let every man fight the good fight in his own calling. If you are a man or woman and say to yourself: I will fulfill my ministry; I will not run away into a monastery, but will do the work God has given and seek no other, you are fighting the battle. If you are a husband or wife, you have your calling from God, and so have the servant, the maid, and the mayor." [11]

"We must always keep in mind that the sinner relinquishes all claims to goodness. We live under the forgiveness of sins. The unpretentious sinner has vastly more potentialities than the proud saint." [12] For the Christian on earth will ever be *simul iustus et simul peccator*, simultaneously a sinner and a just man.

"Because Jesus Christ is his Lord, the disciple's vocation is determined by the need of the neighbor which must be met. To love God and to love this neighbor becomes one command and one love. . . . The Lord, who has freed him, now guides his decisions in the use of his freedom and opens the way through them to a more perfect freedom. This freedom is meant to pervade every mundane task, all the various labors of all Christians: husband and wife, employer and employee,

---

[11] Luther, p. 299.

[12] *Work and Vocation*, ed. John Oliver Nelson (Harper), p. 71.

king and subject. The place in which a person is called is the place for realizing his freedom. . . . In whatever work the disciple may be engaged, he can with this help serve without bitterness, fight without hatred, pray without ceasing, give thanks without reservation, rejoice without fear, love without self-concern, hope without anxiety." [13]

Luther believed that, no matter what one's social status might be, one has an opportunity to serve God. And by serving his neighbors, the Christian fulfills his *Beruf,* or calling, or vocation. "There is no such thing as a profane or merely secular vocation from which God is absent and in which God cannot be served."

"What Luther has done is to dignify the whole body of natural and necessary human services. To carry out work in this temper is to express one's love for one's neighbor and at the same time to fulfill one's obligations under God. This is nothing less than a revolutionary 'transvaluation' of medieval values. Luther was nowhere more truly the pioneer of a modern understanding of man." [14]

Accordingly Luther seems to have changed or adapted the idea of vocation from Johann Tauler and other medieval mystics, who felt that any man or woman, not only a monastic, might have a vision of perfection. But these mystics felt that such a vision of perfection would more likely come to a faithful follower of the monastic way. Luther swept all this aside and said that the *vocatio,* or *Beruf,* is applicable to the entire sweep

---

[13] *Work and Vocation,* p. 108.

[14] Robert Lowery Calhoun, *Lectures on History of Christian Doctrine.* Yale Divinity School. Privately printed.

of civil and political activity. That one was called to serve in an office regarded as spiritual or holy does not mean that the works one did in such a position earned a superior rating before God.

Luther steadily maintained the principle that what God has created is good. Men who are engaged in the natural pursuits may be regarded as doing that which is good, since God has ordained them. Luther said that God requires the same whole-souled dedication of all men. But as Einar Billing warns: "Never imagine you have rightly grasped a Lutheran idea until you have succeeded in reducing it to a simple corollary of the forgiveness of sins." [15]

[15] Philip S. Watson, *Let God Be God* (Muhlenberg).

Chapter 3

WHAT IS WORK?

IN order to appreciate and to understand the implications of our Christian attitude toward our calling, it is necessary to study the concept of work. The variety of definitions of the word *work* indicates that many people have different concepts of work. Is playing tennis work? Does the man who clips coupons from his bonds work? Does the artist who paints a lovely painting work? Someone has said that how you define *work* depends on where you're sitting.

THE DEFINITION

One definition of work is "what we do regularly for pay." This definition is too narrow. Frequently work is done without pay, and yet it is work in the sense of the expenditure of energy. There are other definitions of work, definitions which involve one's relation to society. One expert feels that nothing is truly work unless it makes a contribution to the general welfare of people, but this definition leaves out expenditures of energy that are no contributions to the welfare of society. Is the jeweler who designs an expensive brooch making a contribution? There are those who say he is not.

Perhaps the definition most suitable for our purpose is this one: Work is any expenditure of physical, mental or spiritual energy toward a desired goal. Thus a composer thinking hard on how he might best arrange the harmonies in his symphony is expending mental energy toward the goal of a completed symphony. A machinist at a lathe who manipulates a piece of unyielding steel works because he expends both physical and mental energy to achieve a tolerance of only a thousandth of an inch. One who participates in sports as an amateur or a professional works.

The Christian expends spiritual energy when he obeys St. Paul's admonition to the Philippians: "Work out your own salvation with fear and trembling, for God is at work in you, both to will and to work for His good pleasure" (Phil. 2:12, 13, RSV).

It ought to be obvious, too, that if work is energy directed toward a goal, that goal must be a worthy goal, one that is not out of harmony with any divine standard. The matter of goals in our work will be treated at greater length further on in this essay.

No doubt most Christians at some time or other find themselves in the position of the high school lad who, upon being told by his parents that he would be expected to earn his own living by working, plaintively asked, "Isn't there an easier way to make a living?" Perhaps many Christians feel like echoing the sentiments of Ecclesiastes: "For what hath man of all his labor, and of the vexation of his heart, wherein he hath labored under the sun? For all his days are sorrows, and his

44

travail grief; yea, his heart taketh not rest in the night. This is also vanity." (Eccl. 2:22, 23.)

"Most of us, as we come from office or shop, are vulnerable to this mood. We may suppress sternly any inner resentments against our lot. We may sublimate our frustrations into harmless hobbies or personal hostilities, into gay follies or feverish activities. Yet the awareness of futility keeps gnawing away at our minds. We cannot avoid a taste of bitterness whenever we measure our labor by the cost in effort and the return in joy. This bitterness springs from a deep instinct, from an inborn expectation that toil should yield more satisfying results." [1] Or, as Ecclesiastes states: "There is nothing better for a man than that he should eat and drink and that he should make his soul enjoy good in his labor" (Eccl. 2:24).

IS WORK DREARY?

The first indication we have in the Bible that work is tied up with the problem of sin occurs in Gen. 3:17 (RSV): "And to Adam He said, 'Because you have listened to the voice of your wife, and have eaten of the tree of which I commanded you, You shall not eat of it, cursed is the ground because of you; in toil you shall eat of it all the days of your life; thorns and thistles it shall bring forth to you; and you shall eat the plants of the field. In the sweat of your face you shall eat bread.'" The curse of God strikes the soil, not because the soil and its fruits had sinned but because man had sinned. Only through the expenditure of toil can man eat of his bread. His work will be accompanied by

---

[1] *Work and Vocation*, ed. John Oliver Nelson (Harper, 1954), p. 32.

45

disappointments and heartaches. Frequently there will be no rewards, and frequently the work will seem endlessly toilsome. The original perfection has left the world.

Does this passage say that work is a curse? Obviously it is not in itself a curse, but the hardship connected with it is the consequence of sin, or a curse. Now man's efforts bring but relatively meager or imperfect results. The joy and happiness present in the Garden of Eden has vanished. In that glorious period man knew that he was working in a perfect relationship with God. Now there is tension between man and God. God is angered over man's violation of His laws. Man no longer stands unashamed before God. He is a sinner.

Surely, it ought to be obvious that work can still be a curse in our time. The applicability of this passage to 20th-century conditions is apparent. Work "is a curse when it is meaningless. Then it becomes an intolerable tedium, deadening the mind and embittering the spirit, like the labor of convicts in a chain gang set to breaking rocks all day. It is a curse when it is done under compulsion for ends which the worker hates and against which he inwardly rebels. . . . Work may still seem to many people at least in part a curse when it exhausts the energies and leaves the worker too tired to enjoy his life." [2]

Many moderns, as they contemplate the dreariness of their work, its obligations and its monotonies, become resentful. As they contemplate the prospect of work, they shudder and wish no one had ever mentioned work. They scheme and dream of ways to avoid doing work.

---

[2] *The Interpreter's Bible* (Abingdon-Cokesbury), I, 511, 512.

They want the rewards of work — recognition, success, material satisfactions — but they shudder at the thought of slogging, hard work.

In a novel the heroine's father asks his daughter: "Tell me, Marjorie, what is it in life that's so worth having?" Marjorie replies: "All right, I'll tell you. Fun is worth having. And love. And beauty. And travel. And success." [3]

And Marjorie is convinced that she can dodge the curse of drab toil and avoid the routine tasks of life. She wants the glamor, but she balks at her responsibilities. She confesses without knowing it that the intolerable tedium of work frightens her. She wants everything out of life except work; for work carries a curse with it.

WORK IS A JOY

But in Holy Scripture work has also a joyful connotation, which indicates that work is honorable, dignified, blessed, a necessity. In fact, the very first verse in the Bible speaks of work. God worked when He created the heavens and the earth. Adam and Eve worked in the Garden of Eden. They dressed and kept it. Nowhere in the Bible is there any indication that work is dishonorable or foolish or degrading. God expects man to work. Indeed, St. Paul lays down this rule: "If any would not work, neither should he eat."

Nowhere in the Bible is the worker held in disesteem because he works at some lowly calling. The slave, the farmer, the tax collector, the prophet, the soldier, all render valuable service. It is the attitude that is of primary importance. When the attitude expressed toward

---

[3] Herman Wouk, *Marjorie Morningstar* (Doubleday), p. 195.

one's own calling or another's is wrong, God becomes concerned and utters words of warning. Undergirding all work is God, the Creator. Therefore behind our work there must be the conscious and grateful acknowledgment of God.

When Solomon was engaged in the great project of erecting the temple, he acknowledged his dependence on God's help in these beautiful words: "Except the Lord build the house, they labor in vain that build it; except the Lord keep the city, the watchman waketh but in vain" (Ps. 127:1). "The urgent question for the carpenter is not whether to build a house, but whether in building it his energies will be properly related to God's purpose." [4] If Solomon built this house of God in order to increase his prestige or to earn special favor from God, then his motivation was wrong. Undergirding his approach to the temple construction is the fact that God must guide his thoughts and actions in the work of construction.

The wrong motivation of work is dramatically illustrated in Jesus' parable of the rich fool who harvested a bountiful crop and decided to build larger barns to contain the bounty. He rejoiced over his own ability as a farmer and had no thought of giving God the credit for the magnificent harvest. His unawareness of his responsibility to God brought this drastic sentence: "Fool! This night your soul is required of you; and the things you have prepared, whose will they be?" (Luke 12:20, RSV.)

In his exposition of this verse Martin Luther writes: "This does not mean that He [God] forbids you to work.

---

[4] *Work and Vocation,* p. 41.

Work you should and must, but do not ascribe the fact that you have food to eat and that your house is furnished to your work, but to God's grace and blessing alone. For where it is ascribed to man's own work, covetousness and worry immediately raise their heads and the thought that much work will mean many possessions. Hence the strange contradiction occurs that some who work extremely hard have scarcely enough to eat, while others who work leisurely are blessed with all good things. This means that God will have honor, for He alone makes things grow." [5] "Our works are God's masks, behind which He does all things." [6]

Work is the means God has given us to earn a living. We do not sit in an easy chair, expecting food, clothing, housing, and our luxuries to be handed us on a platter.

Martin Luther has pointed out that we are to regard our work as having a triple value:

1. My work helps to discipline me. The weariness and monotony of life's tasks can drive me closer to God.
2. My work can help me serve my neighbor.
3. My work can contribute to community life, and my work can thus actually make the world a better world to live in.

Work is a necessity. If we do not work, we are drones, and society has its way of punishing drones. Aside from this fact, it is apparent that work must be regarded as more than just something we must do to

---

[5] *Day by Day We Magnify Thee*, trans. Margarete Steiner and Percy Scott (Muhlenberg), p. 297.

[6] *Day by Day*, p. 298. Exposition of Psalm 147.

feed and clothe ourselves and to discharge our various social responsibilities.

Our work makes us utilize our God-given potentialities. Our talents are greater or smaller, fewer or more, than those given to others. But do we use these talents fully? '

I suppose every parent at one time or other is faced by his teen-age son or daughter and told: "Dad, if you really wanted to, you could be earning twice as much money. You're just sitting contented and not doing everything you can." It is at such moments that the conscientious parent wonders whether he has accepted to the fullest extent all the challenges inherent in his job and whether he is truly using every talent he has. He ought to be reminded once more that in a world where God is working out His purposes in Christ any work done at His command, according to His will and to His glory, helps fulfill those purposes. He is a "success," although not according to worldly standards, which his children may unconsciously reflect.

Yet honest self-examination is extremely important. Do I work that extra half hour which might be the decisive factor in this job? Have I explored this possibility or that as far as I can? Have I asked God's help in tackling some particularly difficult problem in my job? Do I keep my eyes open while I'm at work?

However, there are only a limited number of challenges in a job. The coroner who makes autopsies all day long would be hard pressed to see what else he could do in his job. The bookbinder may not be able to see beyond the limited number of operations required to bind a book. On the other hand, one would have to be a dull drudge indeed not to be able to see at least one or two areas in which his job offers him indirect opportunities or challenges.

When the Chicago *Sun-Times* interviewed workers this past winter on the Ford assembly line, a worker engaged in a particularly monotonous job said that after he had mastered his job, he utilized the opportunity to think through plans on how he might improve relationships between labor and management within the factory. A punch-press operator said that he did not permit his mind to be idle while his hands went through the automatic motions. He thought on how he might improve himself as a leader in a neighborhood boys' club which was sponsored by his factory.

Work is a joy. This is not to deny that work has some drudgery. Even the most glamorous jobs reach certain plateaus where the worker must slog on earnestly, committing his time and energy to a dozen different petty details. A job free of drudgery might almost be held suspect. Even casting for trout as regular work would have its dull moments. There are no jobs without their daily grind. Other kinds of work often only seem less wearisome.

But, basically, work can and should be a joy, particularly to the Christian, who works with the knowledge that he has a direct responsibility both to God and to the neighbor. There is genuine joy in doing a job well. I recall a garbage collector who did not bang the cans around; he replaced the covers, and left no debris behind. When asked why he was so different from the usual run of garbage collectors, he replied: "It's fun doing a good job. Why shouldn't I do the best I can?"

He found joy in his work and, I suppose, challenge

and opportunity also. Why? He was serving his community and his neighbor well in a very important service.

Perhaps today, in an age when there is much disquiet and discontent, we should stress the virtue of doing a job well, to the best of one's ability. There is joy in striving for perfection — whether in writing sermons, or making a set of slipcovers for the frayed living-room furniture, or grinding the valves in the car. Knowing he must eventually give an account to God and desiring to serve his gracious Lord, the Christian ever endeavors to do his work faithfully.

FIND THE RIGHT JOB

To find joy in work one must choose a job which will bring satisfaction and opportunity to utilize one's talents.

A Christian can easily make several mistakes in selecting his lifework. A common error many young people make when they select their life's career is that they choose a type of work which will bring them a high salary. Wanting good pay is not wrong in itself. But the person who chooses a career with this one objective in mind is selfish and indicates thereby that his approach to life is governed by materialistic motives.

Another mistake is to look for a great deal of glamor. Many young people look longingly toward Hollywood or Broadway because they feel that there they will be in the spotlight with all eyes on them. This again is a purely selfish reason for choosing a job and is disturbing proof that such an individual is highly egocentric in selecting a calling. There is nothing wrong in wanting to be a great actor or a star at the Metropolitan Opera, but if self-glorification is the motive, it is not Christian.

Don't choose a job simply because it offers security. Some young people say, "I will choose this job because I'll never get laid off and because I'm sure of a pension at 60 or 65." Choosing a job merely because it seems to offer economic security in old age reveals a poor sense of stewardship. And, after all, is there absolute security in this world?

Again, others choose certain jobs because they seem to be easier than others or involve no risks or are less demanding on one's time and energy. It's possible to find jobs which will pay you well for a forty-hour work week plus vacation with pay. But is this the only reason why one chooses a certain job?

What criteria ought one to use, as a Christian, in choosing his life career? The following four check questions will serve as a guideline to one who wishes to give advice to a young person undecided on his lifework or seeking to evaluate his job:

Can I serve God in my work? The job you choose must never be one which in its very nature violates God's laws. This principle automatically eliminates all jobs which involve sinning. A bookmaker for a race track or a faro dealer in a gambling house is obviously occupied in a job which violates God's standards. On the other hand, the type of job you choose should open to you ways of serving God, of witnessing to Him through action and through word. There are certain jobs which expose a Christian to temptations far more easily than do other jobs. There are also jobs that would make it exceedingly difficult for you to offer an effective witness to your faith. Naturally, if you feel that with God's help you are able to remove these roadblocks to the confession of God's name, then you are certainly entitled to choose such a job. But be perfectly aware of the difficulties connected with such a job before choosing it as a life career.

Can I serve my neighbor in my work? The love of God and the love of your neighbor are closely and inseparably intertwined. If you love God as He would have you love Him, then you will also love your neighbor. Therefore the restrictions or qualifications set up in the first question apply with equal force in this matter of serving your neighbor. Practically every job among the 21,000 legitimate job choices available is one through which you will have an opportunity to serve your neighbor, to show love to him. The riveter on a skyscraper who works for the love of God and his neighbor will take special pride and care in his job, knowing that if he is careless in his task, someone may someday on that account be killed. There are some jobs in which the opportunities to serve your neighbor are not so immediate. If you wish to be of greater immediate service to your neighbor, then select an occupation which will bring you into direct contact with many people.

Is the job I choose in harmony with my faith? As a Christian you have chosen to follow a certain path, the path to God through your Savior Jesus Christ. You have standards of conduct which are different from the standards of the non-Christian. One standard you have is that you serve God in your calling. You believe that God has called you to this particular place in life. If you choose a job in which you are required, directly or indirectly, to do that which is contrary to your conscience, then you will find yourself in a difficult position. You may compromise your faith. You may violate your conscience. This is not to say that there are jobs in the world immune to temptations. Whether you are a bricklayer or a consecrated missionary, temptations to do wrong will come. But remember that the job in itself should not force you to live and to act in disharmony with your faith. Choose a job which will give you every opportunity to live and work according to the dictates of your conscience.

Have I chosen the calling for which I am best suited? God has given everyone a talent. This may be a humble, small, almost minute talent. On the other hand, you may have a wide variety of talents. God has imposed on you the stewardship of these talents. He does not want you to waste them. He requires that you give an accounting. The boy who is brilliant in science and seems to have an almost sixth sense in solving the most abstruse chemical equations and then decides to become a plasterer, because it is an easy choice to make, is not making full use of his talents. The girl who has a special knack in designing clothes, and is encouraged by her teachers to become a designer, but decides instead to sell tickets in the local movie theater, is wasting her talents.

SPECIFICALLY

Adults who are placed in the position of advising young people in this matter of career selection frequently wonder how they may best give advice which is consonant with a Christian approach. Here are a few suggestions worth presenting to the thoughtful consideration of the puzzled young person:

Ask God for help. The Christian always asks God for help in making an important decision. Prayer is to be used not only when one is in trouble but also when one seeks guidance in all matters of daily living. Prayer should be earnest conversation with God. Bring your questions and your unsolved problems to God. Ask Him to direct you in your choice. Solutions may frequently occur to you as you talk things over with God in prayer. Sometimes the answer may come quickly; at other times, after a long wait. Of this much you may be certain: God will hear you and will answer your prayer in His way in His time. His answer will always be the right answer.

Study yourself before choosing your job. Just what kind of person are you? Do you get along well with people? Are you inclined to be moody? Are you easily discouraged? Do you like the challenge of difficult tasks? Are you inclined to be lazy? Be honest with yourself. If you want to be really painstaking, make up a check list and measure yourself against it. There are any number of books and pamphlets designed to help you. Ask your teacher for a check list which you can use privately.

If you know that you like to be with people and get along well with them and like to be of service to them, then you will not choose a job which requires you to be alone on some difficult research job.

Use people in helping you to choose your job. Your pastor is interested in you. Discuss your problem with him. His wide range of experience will be placed at your disposal. He knows you well. He is not only interested in you; he also loves you. Talking over your problem with him will help you clarify some of your own thinking.

Use your parents. After all, they are profoundly concerned about your future. They have nurtured you; they have been concerned about your religious training and your education. While there may be some parents who will insist on choosing their child's future career, most parents will hesitate to force their own decision in such an important matter.

Use your school counselors. Most high schools have one or more teachers whose specific task is to guide the students into the proper careers. They have at their finger tips many resources to help you. They have information on job opportunities. They will be able to tell you the educational requirements of various jobs.

In addition to the advice of your school counselors, you can take a variety of tests. These tests, while not always final, do indicate a general trend and show you in a general way where you might be most successful. Dr. G. Frederic Kuder has developed such a series of tests, and your high school teacher will be happy to tell you about them. But it is important to remember that the results of these tests are not final. A test may show you to have the potential of becoming an excellent research chemist, but you are determined to be a cattle breeder. If that is what you want and you feel you have the resources to become a cattle breeder, then nothing should stop you. Therefore use your common sense.

Seek opportunity to talk with people who are already at work in the particular vocation you want to choose. If you want to become a tree surgeon, talk with some tree surgeons in your community. Find out why they like their jobs, what the requirements are, what the good or bad points about the job may be. If you are wavering between several vocations, talk with the people who are now in them. Suppose you are undecided whether to become an accountant, a lawyer, or a social worker. Make it a point to talk with the people in your community who are in these vocations. They will be willing to give you the information you want, and they will be delighted to have a young person come to them for advice on choosing a career.

Read about the jobs you are interested in. Your school or public library will have a variety of books which discuss the particular occupations to which you feel attracted. The librarian will give you further information on books to read. The more you become acquainted with the many aspects of a job, the less you will drift toward a choice. You will reach a point at which you can make a decision. Once having made that decision, you can begin shaping your studies, your part-time work, and your thoughts toward the day when you will be a full-fledged worker in the calling you have chosen.

Chapter 4

THE CONFLICT BETWEEN THE CALLING
AND THE CHRISTIAN FAITH

A faro dealer, an operator of a house of ill fame, or a safecracker are engaged in activities that are in direct contradiction to Christian faith and ethics. Surely, there can be no justification for such occupations. The line of demarcation between right and wrong becomes thinner when the total implications of certain callings are studied and evaluated in the light of Christianity.

At what point does a stockbroker with his manipulations of the market begin violating the Christian standard of love toward a neighbor whom he may possibly hurt through such manipulation? How does a Christian console himself as he goes about his task of making warheads for torpedoes? Does he simply dismiss the matter by saying that his government has need of these devices for the protection of the nation? What about the Christian banker who must foreclose a mortgage on a farmer who has tried desperately to meet the payments? How

may one reassure the judge who must grant one divor
after another to couples who have no Scriptural groun
for obtaining a divorce?

WHAT'S YOUR PROBLEM?

There are five general areas of modern life in whi
the Christian finds himself in vocational dilemmas of t
most disturbing kind.

Our business or industrial society stresses the i
portance of competition, the necessity of production
more goods, and the depersonalization of the work
Many times a businessman will find that because
corporation demands a certain procedure in increasi
production and meeting competitive demands, he w
be forced into a course of action which will harm so
of his neighbors. This is not to argue that competiti
of itself is evil or that the production of more goods
to be deplored. But unfortunately, these are apt
become the end rather than the means of providing t
greatest good to the greatest number of people.

Suppose a businessman or an industrial worker
forced by the nature of his job to perform a task whi
in itself is not a violation of the Christian code, b
which in its implications will hurt people. Won't he fe
disturbed about it? Where is he to go for guidanc
If he approaches his employer, he may meet with a sy
pathetic response, but he may also be ticketed as o
who is queer or one who takes his religion too serious.
His chances for promotion will be jeopardized, for
personnel manager will seriously consider a man who
ethical values question a company's policies.

"There is a true contemporary story," Elton Trueblo
relates, "of an advertising man in a great American ci

60

whose special assignment was the promotion of a certain whisky. He was a skilled man in his profession and knew how to make the product appealing to prospective customers. As a result of his ability and success he was well paid and had built up for his suburban home a high standard of living expense. Many, in the light of secular standards, would consider such a man an outstanding success. But the day came when the man began to lose respect for himself. He was convinced not only that his advertising was harmful; he was convinced that it was also insincere. He labored mightily to convince readers and hearers that his client's whiskey was better than others of its type while he felt sure in his own heart that the whole claim was a lie. Consequently, he went home one day and announced that he was through and, to the amazement of neighbors and friends, he began to engage in productive work that brought in only a fraction of the income of his former position. He did all this because the idea of Christian vocation had gone deeply into his life." [1]

A dilemma of another kind is indicated by the action of Theodore Quinn, who was vice-president of the huge General Electric Company. Its president, Gerard Swope, told Quinn that before many years Quinn would be his successor. Yet Theodore Quinn, still in his early forties, handed in his resignation with this explanation: "I began to realize that I was serving no socially worthwhile purpose in helping a giant to become even bigger." He was upset because he felt his company was interested in growth solely for growth's sake, that the corporate interest created an air of impersonality and thus men

---

[1] *Your Other Vocation* (Harper), p. 72.

became mere pawns in the development of the company
policy.[2]

This may be a dark-toned picture. Nevertheless
does point up a dilemma which must confront thousand
of responsible Christian businessmen.

I do not mean to single out the businessman alon
for the worker in the modern business or industrial worl
has problems equally disturbing. Frequently the Chri
tian member of a labor union will be disturbed by a d
cision of his union. Slowdowns, work stoppages, strik
may be the decision of the majority of the union, b
the Christian workers, who may be in the minority, wi
disagree. What is the Christian to do? Quit his jol
Argue with the shop steward or with the business agen

Even though we speak of an industrial society, w
cannot forget the Christian farmer who is confronte
with decisions which will violate his conscience. Sha
he accept subsidies from the government? What is to l
his attitude toward price-support plans? Must he co
form to a government decision to reduce his herd or h
acreage? If he does not abide by a government decisio
he may well find himself in a vulnerable position.

The Christian men in the armed services of the natio
many times discover that they are forced to accept dec
sions from their superiors which are not at all in harmon
with the Gospel. They dare not disobey, because di
obedience will not be understood or the reasons for suc
disobedience will not be clear-cut.

As an illustration of how the modern fighting ma
may find himself in a painful dilemma, consider th

2 Marquis W. Childs and Douglass Cater, *Ethics in a Busine
Society* (Mentor Library), p. 90.

account. Recently some Hiroshima maidens arrived in this country to receive treatment for their hideously scarred faces and bodies, the result of our dropping of the atom bomb on Hiroshima on August 6, 1945. Brought over to the United States with the help of conscience-stricken American citizens, these twenty-five maidens have received treatment which will improve their appearance and make them more willing to face society. This project has aroused the interest of many people. Most significant, however, was a telephone call received at the office of the *Saturday Review,* May 14, 1955, whose editor, Norman Cousins, was one of the men responsible for bringing them over. The man identified himself as Robert Lewis. This is what he said: "I just wanted to say how personally grateful I am for this project. I was the captain of the plane that dropped the bomb."

Since early childhood days most of us have been solemnly advised that time is money. The example of the industrious man who uses every second of a busy day is held before our awe-struck eyes. This is not to decry such advice even though it is given from a pragmatic point of view. The truth is that time is a gift, a certain allotment of a stewardship responsibility which we must utilize. It is therefore a question with the conscientious Christian how he may best use his time without appearing to fritter away opportunities. This is especially so because often his calling demands a commitment of minutes and hours which ultimately deprives him of time for establishing or re-establishing spiritual relationships.

The modern church needs the time of laymen merely from an administrative point of view. Congregations, districts, and synods have budgets which run into the hundreds of thousands, yes, millions of dollars. Good stewardship demands that prudent and decent business standards be used in the administration of these funds. This requires time. Shall time be taken from the calling which provides the lay member with his wages, or shall the church be denied his help and advice?

His calling as a Christian requires a worship life which reaches its weekly peak in attendance at divine worship. All too often companies require Sunday work or may demand that meetings of a serious nature be conducted during the hours when the congregation meets for its worship service. It is a tribute to thousands of Christian businessmen that when confronted with such a dilemma, they are ready to forsake the demands of their secular calling and present themselves in the congregation for the Sunday morning worship.

The drive of modern life, the increasing feeling of nervous tension in young and old, the pressure of meetings of special interest groups, have caused the slackening of interest in family devotions. The family can no longer be held together long enough for family devotions because other demands split up the family. Private devotions are rarer because many Christians are so utterly exhausted by the demands of the day that they totter into their beds with the half-spoken thought: "Thank God, another day is past! How did I ever make this one?" Perhaps this explains the phenomenal interest in the recent novel by C. S. Forester, *The Good Shepherd,* whose hero, a destroyer commander during World War II, finds time every night to kneel by his bunk and say his prayers. Modern man looks at him incredulously.

Someone has remarked that the age of private life

is over. We are far more conscious of our relationships with the people not only of our community but also of all parts of the world. We are becoming increasingly aware that what happens to the people in Indochina affects us. The rate of pay of miners in the Belgian Congo is of immediate concern to all of us; for those miners unearth most of the uranium which our country needs to produce the A-bomb and the H-bomb.

And so in our calling as political and social entities we find ourselves confronted with problems, with puzzling situations, and with ethical dilemmas. Perhaps some of us, in our particular church denomination, are today more painfully aware of a change in attitude than in past years. Sociologists have pointed out that one church's "attitude toward society tended to encourage passivity rather than social reform. This encourages an admiration of things as they *are* rather than of things as they may *be*. Because of man's incorrigibility and original sin, the [member of this denomination] has little optimism as to the possibility of social improvement, particularly in the secular sphere. . . . [This denomination] has been somewhat indecisive as to how much it wanted to become involved in the world, because if one was to get into the world, he might somehow become part of the world."

John Donne said no man is an island, and thereby he pointed up once more that the Christian's vocation as a citizen is a demanding one, even though it may involve him in ethical dilemmas. It is therefore desirable that the Christian become a precinct committeeman; that he know ward politics; that he understand the operations of the water commissioner's office; that he explore the relationships between organized crime and the local police department. Polite aloofness or unconcern is too dangerous a course to follow in an age which is torn apart by rival claims of varying political philosophies.

There is nothing more discouraging than to hear a group of Christians dismiss the actions of Congress as "sheer politics." It is not enough for a Christian to say that he will bear arms for his country should the need arise. He should also try to understand why his party chairman in his township accepted the gift of a new Cadillac from a contractor. Is the party chairman dishonest? Whose fault is it that a Chicago alderman sells driveway permits? Does a Christian ever wonder why slot machines flourish in one ward but are not found in another? How can slums be permitted to stand when building inspector after building inspector condemns the wiring, the plumbing, the room subdivision? Or perhaps the Christian as a citizen ought not to meddle in these matter lest he become tainted?

When John G. Simmons ran for mayor in Minneapolis several years ago, he was roundly defeated. Analyzing the reasons for his defeat after a vigorous campaign in which he attacked civic corruption, Mr. Simmons said: "The chief moral decisions and ultimate loyalties of Christians are determined by the political, economic, and social groups to which they belong, and not by their faith, life, or church." Perhaps the candidate was harsh in his judgment. Perhaps the Christian voter was torn between loyalty to an alderman who was genuinely concerned about adequate garbage collection, but was not too careful in his associations with the underworld, and a mayoralty candidate who spoke in lofty, idealistic terms.

The brilliant junior U. S. Senator from Oregon, Richard L. Neuberger, summarized the problem of political activity on the part of respectable people when he wrote:

> The government may decide whether we go to war, what kind of public schools our children attend, the condition of business and agricultural economy, even the preservation of the resources on which we rely for sustenance and livelihood. Yet the bulk of our citizens feel neither the desire nor the duty to participate in government. This is something left for the other fellow to do. All too often "the other fellow" turns out to be a person who should not be controlling our destiny in the legislature, congress, or city hall.
>
> I have sat around the fireside while my friends told of the hopes for their sons. They wanted their sons to be doctors or farmers or pastors or bakers or mechanics. This was well and good. Finally, a mercant said unconcernedly that he trusted his son would decide to go into politics. There was a titter in the corner of the room. Several people looked embarrassed. A hiatus occurred in the conversation. It was obvious that the merchant's remark had evoked consternation and sympathy. The others felt the son of the storekeeper was bound for politics and thus, perhaps, for perdition. Yet the merchant's son, if he attained his goal, might thrust the other sons into uniform, tax them into bankruptcy, or blunder them into an economic depression.
>
> The episode was fresh evidence of the fact that 69 per cent of Americans have indicated they definitely do not want their children to be politicians. . . . There is a feeling abroad in the land that politics is

not quite respectable, that it is something which people of probity just don't go in for.[3]

Besides being interested in the local and national community, the Christian is concerned about his responsibility toward all people. Whether it is the Point-4 Program, the United Nations, or the earthquake which destroys homes and lives in a distant spot, the Christian feels involved and obliged to help the unfortunate. At this point in history the sensitivity of the Christian is an asset to be cherished by every nation.

At the same time, how is the Christian as a citizen to solve the moral dilemmas in which his government often places him? In World War II a group of Germans were involved in the bomb plot on Hitler's life. Who is to decide whether they were right or wrong in attempting to assassinate the head of the state? Their leader had involved the nation in bestial practices. They felt responsible as citizens. Was this the way to resolve such a dilemma?

WHAT IS IMPORTANT?

The closest of all social relationships is the family unit. Children, parents, husbands, and wives are bound together in a close-knit union. The difficulties of being a Christian parent today hardly need a lengthy exposition here. Parents do have a Christian vocation as fathers and mothers. Here God has placed them, and here they are to exercise their calling.

But the difficulties facing the modern Christian parent drive many to despair. These difficulties may be both in the area of providing sufficient income for a growing

---

[3] *Adventures in Politics* (Oxford), p. 62.

family and in the area of proper disciplining of the children. No parent who deals with adolescent children in the home will readily confess that it is a joyful task, because adolescents occupy a world of their own, one often antagonistic to the home itself.

As for the economic responsibilities of parents, the solution frequently seems to be to have both partners in the marriage work. One of the astonishing developments of the past few years is the amazing rise in employment of married women. More married than single women are gainfully employed today. As a result, the "doorkey child" is no longer a strange phenomenon of World War II. You have those children today.

Coupled with economic pressures placed on parents to provide home, food, clothing, and transportation is also the pressure to participate in community activities. These activities are, it is readily admitted, necessary for better government, hospitals, schools. Frequently the mothers are the ones who must do the work. When these mothers undertake the fulfillment of what they feel to be their calling as citizens, you have another type of doorkey child. I wonder, too, whether the church is completely guiltless in this matter. I recall one boy's complaint about his mother. He said, "Mother is always working at the church and never bakes cookies and pies." Ostensibly this mother was setting an example to other women, but was she fulfilling her role as a mother and parent? Needless to say, fathers are equally to blame when they are constantly away from the home performing civic and religious obligations and neglecting their own sons and daughters.

When Dr. Herbert Ratner, health commissioner for Oak Park, Ill., stated publicly that the place for young mothers is with their young children rather than with people who engage in a multitude of community enterprises, PTA affairs, and church activities, he was both roundly condemned by the mothers and cheered. One mother wrote in defense of Dr. Ratner to the Chicago *Daily News:*

There are countless willing and sensible parents working to improve the general environment of children in their community and there should be more — but they should be parents of children who have passed babyhood and early childhood.

It is my firm conviction that in the long run a young mother serves her children, her family, and her country best by being there, home, on duty, twenty-four hours a day.

She should be made to feel that she is doing the most important job in the world. As she is.

This young girl is just about as close as you can come to being irreplaceable. She is often filled with uncertainty about her duty — largely because her work is often dull, nerve-racking, and seemingly unrewarding.

It doesn't help her confidence to rush up from doing the diapers to answer the phone and hear that she owes it to her children to be out beating on doors for some worthy cause. To these girls, with all my admiration and love, I give the following recipe:

1 part courtesy — 2 parts firmness — 1 part brevity — serve with the following sentences: 1. I am so sorry; it is not possible for me to help you. Period. 2. Excuse me, I hear the baby. Good-by.

We know that her children will not become community problems, in all likelihood, because she is always there, with a big hug and a smile — going slightly stir-crazy sometimes, but she was home.

Marelen F. Allen
Chicago *Daily News,* May 10, 1955

These, then, are a few of the areas of conflict between one's calling as a Christian and one's calling as a citizen, as a worker, as a parent, as a member of society. It is obvious that many times we as Christians find ourselves in contradictory positions. We want to do what is right, but at the same time we find that pressures of all kinds force us to do things which we know are basically wrong.

CONFESSION IS GOOD

The need, therefore, of a clear acknowledgment of our shortcomings and sins is apparent. We must humbly acknowledge that we have been wretched failures and that we have neglected to do that which God expects of us in our various callings. For many moderns, particularly the contemporary pagan, this is a bitter pill to swallow. A traffic manager for a large corporation said to me: "What is there to repent of? I try to do the best I can. Nobody can expect any more of me." Even the modern Christian feels that repentance is a mood not quite in keeping with modern emphasis on relevant Christianity. There are churchmen who criticized the German Christians after World War II because they called for a national awareness of the need for repentance for the deeds of their nation under the Nazi regime.

But repentance is a necessary part of day-to-day living. Jesus called men to repent, as did His disciples. Generally speaking, repentance means an expression on man's part of deep-seated sorrow and shame over his deeds and thoughts. As man measures himself against the yardstick of God's demands, he realizes he is an abject failure. On the surface man's life may be respectable and totally devoid of crass sinning. Yet by the Law he knows that his life is evil. Man travels a road

71

which leads him away from God. He turns off this road and exclaims, "My own most grievous fault!"

This acknowledgment of guilt and rebellion is one of the most difficult of all processes for the modern. To express a consciousness of sin means the denial of all pride in self. The 20th-century ego simply cannot understand that its accomplishments are tainted with sin and are too often a conscious rebellion against God.

"The decisive question is not how we can manage to avoid wars and disasters, but rather how we stand in God's eyes. Our real threat does not come from pen, 'powers' or the forces of nature, but from God, whose judgment no man can escape. The hidden root of our fear is fear of God, God who will bring to nothing the pride of this world. The important question is this: Is there any deliverance from God's judgment?" [4]

It is apparent that we need God's mercy, which is freely extended to us in Christ. The everlasting truth of grace abounding through the work of our blessed Redeemer brings us comfort in the hours when we feel desperately inadequate.

What is needed in the life of every Christian today is a return to the disciplines of prayer, devout Bible reading and study, and conscientious attendance at divine worship. Alone and dependent on his own resources, the Christian will surely fail.

But the divine comfort of sins forgiven will cause all loads and crosses to become lighter; for God in His omnipotence shoulders all burdens for His children.

[4] Edmund S. Schlink, in his opening address at the Second Assembly of the World Council of Churches, quoted from the *Christian Century,* August 24, 1954.

Chapter 5

YOUR VOCATION AS A WITNESS

It is absurd to accept the facts of salvation and then sit back comfortably, happily complacent because the relationship with God is now perpetually peaceful. Yet that is the reaction of many Christians both individually and as members of a congregation. For such Christians, I suspect, Christianity has become a mathematical formula, something of a supernatural equation which they have tested and found true. Sometimes groups of Christians who regard their faith in such a fashion will band themselves together and dare anyone to breach the wall of their personal satisfaction. They may, figuratively, build a Christian ghetto in which they live snug lives of assurance.

Christianity is a divine imperative: Repent, and believe the Gospel. But *go, tell, do, make,* and *build* are active verbs and injunctions intimately associated with the days of Jesus' active ministry, and obedience to them is a necessary fruit of Christian faith. Our Christianity begets a restless activity. It never stays put in a community or country. It is constantly looking for a way to overcome the impossible or to find areas where it is unknown. Who would have dreamed back in A. D. 33 that some 300 years later the Roman Empire would proclaim Christianity its official religion? Who is willing to say that the Christian faith can be driven out of a nation, as in Soviet Russia, by decree? Such tyranny merely drives the Christian faith underground to keep itself alive in the light of flickering candles.

A professing Christian must share his faith with others. Else he loses his faith entirely; for Christianity cannot be kept in mothballs. If he shares his faith and tries with all his power to tell others about the cross and the open tomb, he makes the startling discovery that his faith gives him renewed impetus, hope, courage. The more you share your faith, the deeper it grows.

Thus it is that every Christian, called of God, is compelled by the very nature of his faith to be a witness. He does his witnessing in a variety of ways: hiring missionaries to go to distant places; distributing tracts; supporting his local congregation and his national church organization; talking with others about Christ. Primarily, however, the Christian has both the challenge and the obligation to witness where he is. In his daily calling, wherever he may be, he may tell others about man's new relationship to God in Christ.

There is extraordinary comfort in the fact that God did not choose the great and the near-great of this world to spread His message. He did not use extraordinary people at the time of Christ. He used ordinary people. As He used them, they became extraordinary people.

Fishermen, tax collectors, housewives, carpenters, soldiers — all familiar occupations — witnessed to the Gospel in Jesus' time. Today God uses salesmen, delivery truck drivers, atomic scientists, pilots, welders, librarians, stenographers — 20th-century people, to spread the Gospel. It is unfortunate that the ordinary Christian so often feels he is a failure as a propagator of the faith because he cannot journey to the Belgian Congo and there preach the Gospel. To compensate for this failure, he will generously support the cause of foreign and home missions, forgetting meanwhile that the personal opportunity and challenge to witness is present in his calling.

THE IONA COMMUNITY

One way of making the Christian vocation real in people's lives is dramatically shown by the Iona Community project, a venture of a group of Scotch Presbyterian Christians under the leadership of Dr. George F. MacLeod.

It had become apparent to churchmen in the busy industrial areas of Scotland that the message of the Gospel no longer had meaning or relevance to the Scots of Glasgow and Edinburgh. Even though the Scotch workingman was a nominal member of the church, it was apparent that actually he had never been in it. "The idea that the family is the basic unit of Christian social living has ceased [in Glasgow] to be true of the middle class, even as it was never true of the working class. And with that change the congregation has lost its roots in the common life of men." [1]

Even more tragic was the fact that devout Scottish Christians lost the sense of missionary enterprise at home. They did not feel they were called to preach the Gospel

---

[1] T. Ralph Morton, *The Household of Faith* (the Iona Community), p. 74.

in the slums of Glasgow nor in the new housing developments outside Edinburgh. At the same time, however, the church turned abroad to preach the Gospel. As one observer noted:

> It may be true that the church found it easier to preach the Gospel to men who were in the primitive rural economy in which the church itself had developed and to which its life was more easily adapted, than to those living in the new conditions of industrial life. It is certain that the idea of the highest Christian vocation came to be interpreted in terms of missionary work abroad and that the conception of vocation as a call to serve God in the secular callings of ordinary life at home was lost.[2]

In order to meet this serious lack in contemporary Christian life, a brilliant young pastor, the Rev. George F. MacLeod of Glasgow, decided to make this entire matter of Christian life and witnessing a reality in the life of his parishioners, many of whom were industrial workers, carpenters, bricklayers, shipworkers. Borrowing a leaf from the monasteries of the Middle Ages, he took over the ruins of Iona, an island of the inner Hebrides, just off the coast of Scotland.

Here was the landing place of St. Columba and his disciples from Ireland, and it soon became the early center of the Celtic Church. In 1938 Dr. MacLeod, together with some of his members, decided to rebuild the ruins of the Abbey Church and its adjoining buildings, which had been dismantled in 1561 at the victory of the Scottish reformers. The object of the enterprise was not primarily the reconstruction of this historic landmark of the church. Dr. MacLeod had in mind that as the men

---

[2] Morton, p. 75.

and women from the mainland worked at the various tasks involving the use of the lands, they would learn that as Christians they might also witness where they are in their daily life back home.

During a three-month period these Christians were indoctrinated with the invaluable lesson that evangelizing was the business not merely of ordained missionaries but also of every Christian. Every believer has the duty and the opportunity to proclaim and demonstrate faith in Jesus Christ. While they worked in the Iona Community, they also learned the great Reformation truths of the priesthood of all believers and that the responsibility of Christianizing or witnessing to the world was theirs. After a three-month sojourn these lay people returned to the factories, city slums, and parish missions on the mainland, ready to carry out the Lord's commission in their everyday tasks as carpenters, bricklayers, accountants, etc.

Thanks to Dr. George F. MacLeod's persuasive eloquence and his personal hard work, this Iona Community venture is no longer an experiment. With each year it attracts more and more lay people from all parts of the world who want to learn everything there is to know about the Christian vocation. It is no doubt due to Dr. MacLeod's work that at the World Council in its 1954 meetings at Evanston the general theme "The Laity — the Christian in His Vocation" was one of the six ecumenical surveys under study. It was the first time in the history of the ecumenical movement that the subject was considered. According to some observers, this section pointed up the fact that Christians are earnestly concerned about bringing their faith into real and daily contact with the workaday world.

Among the youth of the church in America this interest in the Christian vocation is also apparent. Young people perhaps feel the stimulus and challenge of the Gospel in a more striking way than do their elders. Many of them enter the full-time work of the church. There are many thousands who feel the urgency of witnessing to the Gospel. They want to be shown how this may be done as they go about their daily tasks.

In order to demonstrate to young people how to witness to their faith in their daily job, the Walther League, official youth organization of The Lutheran Church — Missouri Synod, embarked on a program with the general theme "Witness Where You Are." Since a merely theoretical approach, through a study program, would not hold the attention of youth very long, it was decided to highlight the "witness" theme in one's vocation by means of a dramatic demonstration.

At the 1954 International Walther League convention in Long Beach, Calif., Leaguers voted to raise a Christian Vocation Fund, which would finance the sending of six volunteer lay workers to the church's mission field in the central highlands of New Guinea. These workers would serve a two-year period without pay. The only compensation they would receive was their travel expenses and a very small monthly allowance. These six workers, to be known as Foreign Mission Builders, were to help in the construction of a hospital, schools, missionary dwellings, an addition to the hydroelectric plant, and other buildings necessary for the mission.

Soon after the announcement of this project was made, the Walther League headquarters received seventy requests for application blanks. After a great deal of screening and careful interviewing, seven, rather than six, young men were chosen. They came from five states and one Canadian province. They represented such diverse callings as farming, carpentry, engineering, students. On April 3, 1955, Palm Sunday, they were commissioned at a service in San Francisco; April 4 they left by plane for New Guinea. By Easter they were at the mission station busily inspecting the hydroelectric plant and worshiping for the first time with the mission congregation.

Their work consisted of a variety of construction projects, working with hammer, saw, plane, level, and other construction tools. They were not in New Guinea for the purpose of conducting Bible classes or teaching in Sunday school. They were laymen working at their calling in this distant land, showing the natives that one can be a Christian in his calling.

Naturally, this project has created a great deal of interest and enthusiasm among the youth; for here they see dramatized the great Scriptural principle that in and through our occupations we have an opportunity to serve God and our neighbor, and, above all, to witness through our life and actions to the glories of the Gospel.

It has caught the imagination of thousands of Walther Leaguers as well as of their parents and their friends. In an age when the dollar reigns supreme it seems almost incredible that seven young men were enthusiastically willing to work without pay in an isolated mission post, far from the comforts of Western civilization. Nevertheless, it is true that seven young men in a special mission endeavor have been pounding nails, sawing, wiring, measuring, and painting to the glory of God.

While the drama of both the Iona Community and the New Guinea project catch the imagination, it is significant that many Christians today have discovered that their calling and witnessing are inseparably tied together. They see that even in the most tedious and humble tasks they can witness through their calling.

Perhaps one of the most common complaints heard from housewives and mothers is that they fail to see the opportunities for Christian witnessing in their vocation and station in life. Claire Sherwood Kimble writes: "Many wives think of themselves only as housewives doomed to a succession of tasks they do not enjoy, kept by their household routine from outside activities or careers that seem more glamorous. They are frustrated because they cannot see the importance of their work. . . . An important problem that every homemaker must solve is raised by the conflict between her desire to care for her family and her concern to minister to the outside world."

Mrs. Kimble feels that a young mother must, in most instances, confine herself mostly to home activities. At the same time, however, her own personal participation in church activities gives her such outlets for witnessing as a prayer group or a choir. Particularly through prayer does she feel that she can make the greatest contribution to a troubled world.

Beyond and above all this activity is the example a Christian marriage and home can set for the community, and ultimately the Christian home will influence the world. "One of the greatest blessings of life is a Christian fellowship between husband and wife. It brings a deeper love, a sacrificial spirit, a bond of understanding not otherwise possible. A woman's role as mother brings her an even deeper awareness of her place in God's plan. When my two sons ask their first questions about God and the stars and growing things; when they encounter unkindness or unfairness; when they experience a moment of beauty, then I know that the answers I come up with are eternally important. It is almost as if I catch a glimpse down the years of their adult lives and understand in part what impact I will have on their lives. Being a mother, her children's best friend and teacher, is an awesome responsibility and a glorious privilege.

"A mother must realize that her children will learn more from what she is than from what she does and says. . . . We are not worried about the answers to future problems. Our Christian faith is our child psychology."[3]

A young engineering salesman in California has captured the joy of the Christian calling as an opportunity to witness on his job. He writes:

I spend most of my time contacting people. These are primarily engineers and, of course, the purchasing agents when it comes time to order. Most of the real selling is on a contract- or production-order basis.

I try each day to utilize the opportunities to witness to my Savior. In my case I try to make it a deliberate and conscious thing. Generally there are three groups of people which I contact. I try to make each group an object of special attention.

The first is the group of people in my office. This is the group I know the best because I have daily

---

[3] Claire Sherwood Kimble, "Homemaking Is My Vocation" (*Christian Century*, June 10, 1953).

contact with them. Actually we depend on each other in a business way, and there are always matters of decision which involve Christian principles.

Frequently on sales trips, while sharing a motel room with one of the fellows from the office, a person finds ideal opportunities to *"tell."* The most startling thing is the sense of values people have. They're looking for security, and they work themselves to death to find it.

Even with the boss it's wise to state your Christian convictions from the start. In my present position it was made clear from the beginning that at no time would I be required to act contrary to Christian principles. Actually a firm resolve on this point has resulted in co-operation by the company and an increased awareness of proper business ethics — and a reason why — the Christian reason.

A clear understanding has made it possible for me to attend church and Walther League functions even though there were conflicting dates. Exhibiting Christian standards stabilizes any office organization. I feel a Christian has an advantage in encouraging rather than compelling the office to get the work out. The people count.

The second group I come in close contact with are the presidents, vice-presidents, sales managers, and chief engineers from the companies we represent. They come out here to visit the various industrial accounts and rely on us to get them around to see the right people. Their very titles indicate that they have, with talent and experience, made a place for themselves in the business world.

I have learned a great deal from these people which I in turn can apply to secular business or in young people's work.

During a two-day period of calling on accounts with the vice-president of one of our Eastern companies I found out that he had been active in a church in his home locality. His wife and children still attended; however, with business pressure as it was, he needed Sunday morning to sleep. So he said. I passed up this obvious opening for the moment because we had just left the Farmers Market in Los Angeles, where he had bought his boy a shirt as a souvenir of California. He was flying home that night, and as I left him at his hotel I remarked, "I surely hope you take your boy to church Sunday in his new shirt." A simple statement, but much different from the one he expected. Usually such good-bys consist in good wishes for more business.

Group three would consist of all the people I call on. As I mentioned, engineers are my primary contact. I even surprise myself sometimes when I suddenly come to the realization, while discussing a technical item, that I'm wondering whether this fellow is a Christian. I think that if I ever really became a success in this calling, it will be because I am anxious to talk, to understand, and to help, if possible, all of those people. Sometimes it's only in a business way, sometimes personally, the Lord willing. My responsibility is to tell. He will do the rest.

Sometimes opportunities are present during the so-called wasted time in a salesman's life — the time when you have to wait in a lobby to see someone. There isn't a receptionist who isn't anxious to talk about last week end, or the week end yet to come, or last night. It's amazing how frequently people actually ask you to tell them about what's most important in your life. Many times only a couple of sentences are said before you're interrupted, but there is usually a next time. People don't forget.

I like direct witnessing. There are many ways to witness without saying a word. Personally, I try to make the openings and let the Lord take over. Certainly, Christians should be good salesmen. We belong to the best company. The President of our company never makes a mistake. It's easy selling. Just tell anyone. He will get the order if He wants it. The salary has already been paid for us. We work out of love. It's great to be a salesman and representative for HIM.[4]

THE SOLITARY CALLING

The subtle interplay between one's calling and one's challenge to witness to the Lord Jesus Christ is sometimes hard to detect. Those who lead lonely lives in solitary callings, such as farmers or research scientists, may wonder how they can make an obvious declaration of faith to the non-Christian. The very nature of their calling is an impediment which bars them from communal living or daily verbal contact with other people.

Harold Blume, a young North Dakota wheat farmer, faced this problem. He found a solution. The way in which he found the solution, and the way in which he carries through as a witness to his faith, sets a challenging pace for all who want to make their Christian vocation and their task as Christian witnesses an inseparable unit. Here is his story:

> I own some good North Dakota land. It is mine. I have a deed in my bank box that says so. A lawyer, my neighbor, and all people will tell you it's mine. It is mine for all human purposes.
>
> But, being a Christian farmer, I know better. It's really God's land. I'm just keeping it for Him. This fact makes me different from all farmers who are not believers in Jesus. I must farm the way He would have me farm.
>
> God is a generous Landlord. He furnishes me the land, the seed, the sun, the rain, the health and strength to farm, and then gives me the whole crop to do with as I please. God surely gets the short end of that business deal. But that's not all. He gives me

---

[4] Bill Sornborger, "I'm a Salesman," in *Walther League Messenger*, February 1955.

the right to sell out or to pass this land on to my sons when I enter the heaven which He has prepared for me through Jesus, the Son of God, my Savior from sin. You see this land I farm for God has come to me in just such a manner from Grandpa to Dad to me.

My church of course is responsible for teaching me the ways of Christian farming. I can see its steeple from my home. It towers high over endless plains that extend from horizon to horizon. It is the center of our community. Here I was baptized, and here my sons were baptized, and God willing, they will attend our Christian day school.

Our church stands 13 miles north of Minot, in the midst of a farming community — grain farming — big farming. The biggest tractors on wheels, the biggest combines, and the biggest tillage implements are found on almost every farm. The machinery has to be big to farm big farms, and the farms have to be big to support a family because this is dry land farming.

Our average annual rainfall is only about 16 inches. If our gracious heavenly Father gives us almost all of it during the growing season, then the crops are well on the road toward a fine yield provided they are not struck down by rust, knocked down to the ground by the sawfly, eaten up by grasshoppers, crowded out by weeds, or beaten by hail or wind. But when our rainfall is short during the growing season, the crops wilt, become stunted, and the kernels shrink.

Of course, the crop is still not a sure thing when it ripens abundantly. It must be swathed — that is, cut down and laid in rows around and around the field. The grain must lie in the swath about a week to dry. During this period wind can easily blow the swaths away, or rain can pound the swath to the ground, which will cause the seed to germinate and grow. Hail can pound the seeds out of the head so that they cannot be saved. Any precipitation will cause the seeds to bleach (losing their fine color and lowering of the test weight).

After the grain has been swathed and is adequately dry, the combine picks up the swath and threshes out the seed. The seed is stored in a granary and later sold.

This seed crop, when sold, is the only pay check of the year for us. On it hinges our year's labor, and oil and gas bills, our machinery repairs and depreciation, our tithe and some of our dreams.

If God should see fit to give us a good crop this year, it means our church will prosper, and perhaps we can help our congregation put running water in our fully self-supporting Christian day school. Perhaps we can put running water in our house; perhaps add a room to our house, which we need so badly; perhaps pay off some of my debt for machinery.

I'm sure you see a farmer's fate is so realistically dependent upon our gracious God. From the time of Jesus' resurrection at Easter, when the grass also begins to come to new life again, and throughout the year our life must needs be a life of prayer. We pray for dry enough weather to get the crop seeded. Then we pray for rain. We pray that no hazards would fall upon our crop if it would so be God's will. We pray for a dry harvest season. We pray for a good price, and we pray for the strength and health to get our work done in season, and we pray that society will distribute the food we produce to hungry people. If the crop is good, Gladys, my wife, and I pray that we may use it wisely to His glory. If the crop be poor, we ask the way to take it lightly and to carry on successfully. After all, the crop is God's and He can surely do with His own as He pleases.

But winter is the time for relaxation and for exercise of the mind. Sometimes we take a trip as we did to the Gulf Coast for two weeks in 1953. In 1952 I took some classes at the college in Minot. Last winter Gladys and I worked on some Correspondence Courses. We read a great deal during the winter and usually spend some time doing repairs on the house that can be done indoors. I milk a few cows, and haul grain, and repair some machinery that can be repaired indoors.

Of course, our winters are sometimes quite severe this far north, but we thoroughly enjoy them just as we do the summers. When snowed in for a few days, one enjoys a solitude, a privacy, and a meditative atmosphere that a city dweller can never experience. When the wind blows and the snow drifts the roads shut, you can easily imagine the face of God sending forth just a small portion of His almighty power and with it so simply transcending the powers and plans of egotistical man. And then when the sun shines through — such beauty — bright sun on glistening snow. Then you see your neighbors again, talk with them, and appreciate people and friends as God would have us do, but which we do so seldom.

Our gracious God has surely given us farmers an enjoyable way of life. We work close to nature, through which God so clearly manifests Himself day to day. Our family can work together in the kind of atmosphere we ourselves build, because we have little interference from the world and wicked people in the world. It is comparatively simple for us to choose Christian friends for ourselves and for our children. We are our own boss, and though we always have work to do, it is still possible for us to leave for a time if we so desire. And all the while we work on the farm we derive a certain satisfaction in that our efforts are directed at growing food for people.

Fully realizing that God gives me as a farmer so much, I understand that of me much shall be expected. Since it is God's land I farm, I must surely take care of it as He would have me do. That means carrying out good soil management and conservation practices so that it will not wash down the river, blow away in the wind, or be "mined" for my personal profit. God has entrusted to me a portion of that soil on which all life depends to use to His glory in a manner that will witness to my neighbors how God would have His land operated.

This is one way I can be a witness for my Savior. To everyone driving down the road past my land that land should witness that it is being farmed as a good steward of God would farm it.

I can be a witness to Him also of course, as every Christian can, by talking about my Savior with all the persons I meet. As a farmer I know something about many skills that can be used for the upkeep and good appearance of my church property. My contribution to a well-kept church and grounds is a part of my witness for Him. When my tractor stands idle on Sunday morning in busy season, that is a part of my witness. My offering on Sunday morning, that is part of my witness, and so are the duties I undertake for my church, my community, and my farm organizations.

I thank God for the privilege of letting me live on the land, that powerful land through which God performs year in and year out the miracle of making food for millions from decayed seeds.

Heavenly Father, show me always that this earth is the Lord's and the fullness thereof. Make me a farmer who walks with God.[5]

THE LIGHTED CANDLE

There will undoubtedly be many times when the Christian in his calling wonders how his witness can ever prove effective or compelling. He may feel that the years go by in a hurried march without ever having given him the opportunity to tell others about the glorious faith of the New Testament which has brought him security. He may feel that the powers of evil and darkness are completely overwhelming. It is precisely

---

[5] Harold Blume, "I Am a Farmer," in *Walther League Messenger,* September 1955.

to counteract this feeling of despair and frustration that Father James Keller launched his famed Christopher movement,[6] which has given lay people new insights showing how they may witness to the world about the Gospel and thus change people's lives. The Christopher motto, "It is better to light one candle than to curse the darkness," is worth remembering when the Christian witness through vocation seems so difficult.

Earle F. Dexter, who has worked with the Indian Americans in the Southwest for many years, tells the story of an old Navaho who gave an effective answer to a white missionary just arrived in Navaho country to start a new mission. The missionary told the old man through an interpreter what his special kind of religion would do for the people.

> The old Indian listened and finally nodded his head. The white man was glad because he thought he had put across his idea with the Indians. Then the old man said: "White man, we would be glad to have your religion do all those things for our people. And it may be that we will all take up with your religion. But we Indians like to know that we're on the right trail before we go too far. So here is what you do: You can settle down and live among our people out here for a long time. We'll watch you, how you live — everything you do. If after a long time we see that the way you live is the kind of life we want to live, maybe we'll all take up your religion. We hear a lot of smooth words from your people, but we have not seen so many whose lives talk. That's what we want to see." [7]

---

[6] Two books by him offer many insights into witnessing and vocation. They are *You Can Change the World* and *Careers That Change the World* (Pocket Books, 25 cents each).

[7] Earle F. Dexter, *Doors Toward Sunrise* (Friendship Press), page 9.

Chapter 6

WORSHIP AND VOCATION

CHURCH membership statistics in the United States are staggeringly impressive. Many commentators feel that the 100,000,000 plus who claim church affiliation offer an overwhelming challenge to atheistic Soviet Russia. Truly, we are ostensibly a nation devoted to God and His ways. The millennium would seem not far distant.

Realistic churchmen are inclined to question these statistics. Quantitively the figures may be satisfactory. No one denies there has been an upsurge in church membership. Qualitatively the figures are not so sound. The disturbing question is: How many of the 100,000,000 attend church on Sunday or the Sabbath (this phenomenal figure includes the Seventh-Day Adventists and the Jews)? Ask any pastor on Monday morning how many of the members on the church roll attended divine services over the week end, and likely, after discounting those who were ill or away on vacation, he will reply, "Forty per cent." More than likely he will say in a moment of candor that the church attendance is downright poor. He will look hopefully at the questioner for a panacea to improve church attendance.

There are those who say that the recent rapid growth of the church in America is the result of the secularization of our society. Dr. David Moberg made a depth study of 104 people who in 1953 joined Baptist churches. Of the main reasons given for joining the church, 44 were predominantly secular, 20 predominantly sacred, 29 "mixed." The others were unclassified. Dr. Moberg stated that the evidence indicated many people joined the church because it offered certain group satisfactions no longer available in other institutions.[1]

Time stated:

America is a spiritual paradox: it is at the same time the most religious and the most secular nation in the world. From 1949 to 1953, U. S. distribution of the Scriptures jumped 140%. In a recent survey of religious attitudes, more than four-fifths of U. S. citizens said they believed the Bible was "the revealed word of God." But another survey shows 53% unable to name even one of the Gospels. And a panel of 28 prominent Americans, asked to rate the 100 most significant happenings in history, ranked Christ's crucifixion 4th (tied with the Wright brothers' flight and the discovery of X rays).[2]

In Protestant churches attendance at a worship service has always been relatively poor. The exceptionally well-attended services are those held on the great Christian festivals, and even some of these, e. g., Trinity Sunday, which marks the beginning of the summer vacation season, may be depressingly poor.

---

[1] *Christian Century,* October 26, 1955.

[2] *Time,* September 26, 1955.

The clergyman frets and fumes. He may resort to scolding those who do attend worship services faithfully and at the same time realize he is not scolding the right people: the absentees. He resorts to a variety of methods to lure the Christians to the regular worship service. He re-examines his sermon techniques, feeling that perhaps out-dated techniques are to blame for the poor attendance. The choir receives a periodic overhauling, and a new organist will be engaged. The new gimmicks of modern advertising and public relations will be applied with a vengeance. The church is redecorated. An active community visitation program is undertaken. Despite all these, and many more, efforts, church attendance may have been increased only from 47 per cent to 51 per cent of the total membership.

The Protestant clergyman and his church board look longingly at St. Rita's teeming congregations attending the three Sunday morning Masses: 7 — 9 — 11. Wistfully the Protestants wish that they could apply some of the pressures which the St. Rita clergy seem to be able to apply to their parishioners. If we could only make it a law to be in church, the church board moans, then this place would be packed every Sunday morning. Of course, there is this to be said about those packed Roman Catholic churches. Many times the St. Ritas will have an 850-capacity church with a 4,000 membership. Filling the church for three masses is no problem, therefore. You may be sure that the Roman Catholic clergy have equally woeful complaints about church attendance.

Why is there such a general disregard of the worship life, both the private and personal worship life, and the public worship life among Protestants generally?

Why do so many churches with a membership of 1,000 consider themselves fortunate if 400 attend the Sunday services?

TAKING OUT THE DULLNESS

Many Christians regard worship as a dull experience indeed. Going to church is a Sunday chore which social custom demands. It is a religious obligation best gotten over as quickly as possible. Despite the attempts of the American Advertising Council to glamorize going to church, too many people still think of the Sunday worship experience as completely unglamorous.

Perhaps some church services deserve such a reaction. The singing is uninspired; the liturgy is depressingly monotonous; the sermons seem irrelevant; the prayers are long and windy. And yet the blame for this feeling of dullness on the part of the worshiper does not lie entirely on the side of the church and its clergy. The vast majority of Christian pastors are deeply concerned about making the Sunday worship life a rich spiritual experience. But they run up against a stone wall because their parishioners do not understand or care to learn about the meaning, the purpose, and the value of worship.

From the days of the early church, in the expressions of the New Testament and in the writings of the early church fathers, the emphasis has always been on the need for Christians to come together to worship. When the church was only an underground movement and when police informers would find their way into the membership, the Christians still felt the divine necessity of coming together for a service of prayer, praise, the Holy Communion, instruction. It was unthinkable not to come together; for these early Christians recognized that one of the essential marks of Christianity was its fellowship expressed in worship. Theoretically those early Christians may have felt that it was possible to worship week after week and month after month alone as they went about their tasks. But in such loneliness there was not the strength that came from being together with their fellow believers.

All of those Christians, as they crept through dark alleys and subterranean passages to meet with the congregation, must have felt the thrill and challenge of the faith. Their faith was charged with the excitement of adventure. The moment they arrived and greeted one another, each must have said to himself: "I am part of this gathering. It cost me risks to come. My life may have been endangered. But it was worth it. Now I shall be stronger." Thus the worship was a shared experience not only in getting to the service but also in participating in all its phases.

The fact is that those early Christians felt in a distinctive way that their worship together was a re-emphasis of the fact that they were living together in a new life which was in Christ. All the phases of their Christian faith only served to reaffirm that they were new creatures. "Theology, worship, and the ministry were necessary to help them live that life and to express to other men their conviction that they were one family called to live that life together." [3]

Throughout the ages the Christian Church has felt it was necessary for the family of believers to come together

3 T. Ralph Morton, *Community of Faith* (Association Press), page 32.

for worship. There were times, in later history, when the church used police pressure to force attendance at divine services. The church was also not above using political, economic, or social pressures. There came a time, too, in the history of the church when worship was no longer a group experience. The believers merely gathered as an audience to witness a select number of Christians of a higher order worship before the altar.

It remains one of the glories of the Reformation that Martin Luther emphatically insisted that all believers must participate actively in worship in order that the values of this group "togetherness" could be thoroughly realized. His development of congregational singing served as a tremendous stimulus to hearten the believer in the knowledge that he was taking part in joint worship with other children of God.

Today some of that early church excitement of danger and the Reformation enthusiasm for worshiping in a group seems to have faded into a halfhearted performance on the part of a group of people who regard attending church as a dismal chore. Who is to blame? Some critics point to the clergy who have forgotten the essential reason for worship; other critics complain that choirs, organists, and even a return to the elaborate liturgical practices of another era have turned the congregation into an audience. Perhaps no one is specifically to blame. Perhaps the hidden disease of spectatoritis has subtly infected clergy and people alike; for this is an age when people sit back impatiently waiting to be amused, enlightened, depressed, excited, or enthralled.

The truth is Christians must realize once more that they are not merely an audience in the church. They do assemble on Sunday morning not to hear of the world nor what the choirmaster has managed to concoct for their edification, but the Gospel of Jesus Christ. Born of God, they want to hear His Word and worship Him who, though unseen, is nevertheless present and waiting for the confessions, the praise, and the prayers of His children. Thus every hymn that is sung, every prayer, spoken or unspoken, every Scripture lesson, and every sermon keeps in mind the centrality of God.

Perhaps modern man will be disconcerted at first when he hears that this is the purpose of his going to church on Sunday or at any other time. This means he will have to toss aside all feelings of egocentricity. He will have to acknowledge that his first obligation is to his Creator, Redeemer, and Sanctifier, the Triune God. Having through the Gospel learned to love God, He will of course also love God's Word and house.

RESPONSE

The idea back of worship is response, the response which man makes to God. This response may take a variety of forms — from the simple worship of a small mission church to the surging dynamism of a great Christian congregation, singing praise on Easter morning. Thus it is no wonder that worship has occupied the artists and poets of all generations. They wish to add to the enrichment of worship.

No worship has value unless it focuses upon one central point: God, unseen in His Person and yet present through Word and Sacrament. The Christian Church insists that, above all, the worshiper must focus his heart and mind upon Jesus Christ. Faith in the Redeemer presupposes that the believer is aware of his unworthiness. His sins stand out in sharply etched form. They become vividly real, and he falls to his knees pleading for mercy. There before the cross the Christian learns that his sins are forgiven. In this forgiveness he trusts and rejoices.

Nothing is more tragic than the confession of a modern businessman who said: "To me worship and going to church always meant confession and forgiveness. In my church the worship service is supposed to give me the opportunity to confess my wrongs. I am supposed to hear the announcement of grace. But there are so many barriers. I forget why I'm in church. I leave the church unsatisfied. Is it my fault? Is it the church's fault? I don't have the answer."

Many Christians, to whom absolution is the key to heaven, will hardly find themselves in a similar predicament. But with them, too, there is room for improvement. Perhaps many of them have forgotten the meaning and value of the liturgy. Few have ever thought to study the rich content of the hymnal. Here is God's plenty for the seeking worshiper. From the opening chord of the confession, "I, a poor, miserable sinner, confess unto Thee all my sins," to the closing benediction, the worshiper, provided he is willing to submerge himself in the dramatic progression of the liturgy, will find himself before the throne of God and will hear the Word of Grace.

Forget for a moment the congregation, those hundreds of others gathered for the same ostensible purpose. Forget the intonations and inflections of the clergyman in the chancel. Forget the hacking and coughing of the congregation. Think first of the personal relationship to God. Once submerged in such an attitude, inevitably there comes the moment when the worshiper is aware that others are doing exactly as he is, that these others also feel their unworthiness, and are awaiting the announcement of grace.

As the worshiper joins the congregation in the chanting of the responses, in the glorious hymns, and in the reverent silence of the prayers, he will find a strength entering his being which comes from the knowledge of peace with God.

Soren Kierkegaard once wrote: "The worship is therefore mingled fear and happiness. Even the most purified and rational worship of God is happiness in fear and trembling, confidence in deadly peril, frankness in the consciousness of sin." [4]

Aside from the general attitude of personal preparation, every worshiper ought to be aware of the magnificent heritage of worship forms bequeathed to the church by preceding generations of the faithful.

The Christian church year begins with the penitential Advent season and sweeps on to the glories of Christmas, thence almost too quickly into the holy drama of Lent and Holy Week, and finally upward to the triumph of Easter and Pentecost. Its very structure is a poignant reminder of the Christian's entire life of faith. No Christian ought to starve his worship life through failure to take advantage of the aid which the church provides him through these sacred seasons and festivals for the enrichment of his personal and group worship life.

The design of the church building serves as a constant

---

[4] Soren Kierkegaard, *Thoughts on Crucial Situations in Human Life* (Augsburg), p. 13.

reminder of the crucifixion; for the chancel, the nave, and the transepts form one gigantic cross within which the congregation assembles. No church is so poor but has at least a series of symbols which spell out pictorially various aspects of the faith. The lamb, the descending dove, the all-seeing eye serve as reminders of the three persons of the Trinity. The symbol of the fish reminds the worshiper of the days when it served as a signal or announcement for the underground church. It was the highway marker pointing to the place of worship. The letters of the Greek word for *fish* are the initial letters of "Jesus Christ, God's Son, Savior." Fixing the eye on these symbols provides the worshiper with one more opportunity to remind himself that he belongs to the long train of faithful who also worshiped. He is in a vast company of the faithful whose prayers have preceded his to the throne of eternal mercy. No thinking Christian can remain unmoved by these reminders.

The colors used in the church vestments and paraments, from the deep violet of penitence to the triumphant and flaming red of victory, serve as signposts along the march of faith toward final victory.

Preparation on the part of the worshiper before he enters the church and awareness of the significance of the liturgy and all parts of the service, imperfect as they may be in their rendering, will help in ridding himself of those petty annoyances which distract or make him feel that worship with the group is meaningless. He will leave the church with the strengthening assurance that he has been in the house or the home where God is present at all times for His people.

Equally significant in the life of the Christian is the time spent in personal worship. A distracted housewife and mother complained to her pastor: "How can I make my everyday life have meaning? Everything I do seems so useless."

The pastor asked: "Have you ever tried to worship God in your home?"

The mother replied: "I knew you would say that. Very well. Tell me how I can worship at home with my family and when I'm alone."

Delighted with the challenge, the pastor said: "There must be others like yourself. Supposing we find a few more people interested in developing their own devotional life in relationship to this business of living. We'll spend a little time together considering some of the techniques. Perhaps after a few hours of discussion, you will obtain insights which may prove helpful."

The mother agreed to the suggestion. In the next weeks a small group of men and women gathered in the pastor's office and discussed under his guidance the various aspects of the personal worship life. There was nothing to startle in the information. There were no new techniques. The discussions did serve as a stimulus for further thinking.

The informal course began with a consideration of prayer, in which the Christian talks to his God. He must recognize with St. Augustine that he is restless until his soul rests in God. Thus "prayer is being in the presence of God. . . . Prayer is the recognition of the power of God, and the realization that we can get power from no other source. It is recognizing that we have no power within ourselves to help ourselves, knowing our utter dependence on God for every good thing. Prayer is opening the heart to God that He may come in; it is letting down the drawbridge which spans the space between us and God. We must let down, but when we do, God crosses over it to us and aids us in crossing back to Him." [5]

Prayer may be in a variety of forms. It may be the confession of sins; it may be the intercession for a sick child; it may be praise and adoration. Prayer may be as varied as the changing seasons and as different as the colors of the rainbow. Prayer is communication between the child and the Father. Prayer is the spoken and unspoken pleading with God. All the life of a Christian can be a prayer, a continual living in the presence of God.

An invaluable aid to the development of the prayer life is cultivating the art of meditation. In an age when every effort is made to distract the human being, meditating may seem a foreign device imported from India, where the drive and energy of Western civilization is an object of wonderment to the serene Indian. Others feel that meditating belongs in some monastery far from the roar of turbojets. Here in lonely cells monks spend their hours in a state of meditative ecstasy.

Meditating is simply thinking. Everyone meditates. The housewife as she contemplates the problem of disobedient Susan meditates about child behavior and parental attitudes and all the other factors which might contribute to disobedience. She weighs all the data and ultimately arrives at a decision. While no involved

---

[5] Constance Garrett, *Growth in Prayer* (Macmillan), p. 4.

thought processes may come into play in this particular situation, yet there is at least some thought.

Most people do some thinking at some time, willingly or unwillingly. Thinking can be a hard chore, as exhausting as operating a drill press in a noisy factory. Thinking, if it is done at all regularly, can contribute to self-discovery and self-knowledge. This can be a disconcerting experience. By and large few people devote much time to thinking, because it is time-consuming and it demands attention. The new points of view which are bound to arise from thinking through a problem or a situation may cause personal confusion.

Meditation is thinking. It has a connotation of calm, devotion, rumination. It is a word used particularly in reference to thinking about God and the things pertaining to God. It involves a listening to God, to His Word. Meditation implies a receptivity which is sometimes absent when pursuing a thought process to its logical conclusion. "Purposeful thinking about God is meditation." [6]

One of the easier ways to discover the joys and values of meditation is to keep three verbs in mind: Look, Think, Resolve. Open the Gospels and study the account of our Lord's visiting Zacchaeus.

Look at Zacchaeus. Picture the setting: the swirling crowd as Jesus pushes His way to the home of the notorious tax collector; the astonished murmurs of the people. Place yourself in the crowd as you watch the progress of the Man from Nazareth. Study the nimble footwork of Zacchaeus, nervous, excited, joyous, unable to grasp immediately the tremendous thrill of this

---

[6] Ibid., p. 88.

moment. Try to understand why Jesus decided to visit the home of a social pariah.

Think about Zacchaeus. Catch the significance of the long-promised Messiah visiting the home of one who had sold out to the conquerors. Why did He do it? Would He visit your home? Would you be willing to invite this Carpenter into your home? Would your home be prepared to receive God?

Resolve to do something as a result of your thinking about this startling occurrence. If it consoles you, have you resolved to bring consolation to some outcast you have heard about or know through personal acquaintance? Have you decided to visit the alcoholic down the street? Will you make your home a place where your Lord will visit you and share your sorrows and joys? "The resolution must be definite, practical, and one that can be carried out, at least in part, that very day. It will have to do with your own life, character, or work in relation to your present surroundings or associates." [7]

What else is there to meditate about besides specific Biblical scenes? There are the miracles of Jesus, His prayers, the disciples, the Psalms, the great creeds of the Christian faith. As the religious imagination is exercised, more and more subjects for meditation will present themselves. No one, making even a halfhearted effort, would ever dare complain of an impoverished spiritual life once he has begun to practice the art of meditation.

Whether one meditates a few minutes a day before praying or an hour, there are bound to come to the

[7] Ibid., p. 92.

seeking individual rich spiritual insights which suddenly make life far more meaningful. Those who cultivate meditation and prayer will find it perfectly natural to breathe a prayer while waiting for the stoplight to change to green. The ancient Celtic Christians prayed upon every occasion in the day's progress from dawn to sunset. The housewife baking her loaf of bread and the farmer scattering the seed in his field breathed short prayers, beseeching heavenly benediction on all aspects of labor. Worship and the Christian calling were part of the fabric of living. Work and worship were inseparable.

There was a time when some Christians observed eight periods of worship during the day. In our time this appears almost incredible. Still if the 20th-century Christian kept in his consciousness the fact that each segment of the day has its particular significance in relation to the Creator, his devotional life would be richer and more meaningful.

There was Matins, celebrated before daybreak, when the believer had the opportunity to meditate upon the divine Word. Then came Lauds at dawn, a time of praise. As nature begins its song, man praises his Creator and Redeemer at the beginning of a new day. Shortly after Lauds comes Prime, the period of supplication. Now man prepares for the day's tasks. He needs the kindly protection of God to guide him through the toil and heat of the day. Now comes Tierce (9 A. M.), Sect (12 noon), and Nones (3 P. M.), short hours in which the believer again and again turns to God asking Him to hallow the day. At the close of day, there is Vespers, and the believer glances back over the hours which God has given him. He has the opportunity to thank God for the blessings of the day. The last hour of the day is Compline, the hallowed hour before the believer closes his eyes in sleep. He peers into the night, which is symbolic of the works of evil, and commits himself trustingly into the hands of his Lord.

In this age of aspirin and automation it may appear slightly ridiculous to suggest to the Christian to observe these ancient canonical hours. Most Christians would be horrified at the thought of devoting this much time to worship. It was Brother Lawrence, of another era, who suggested that it might be well for every Christian to practice the presence of God in his daily life. Thus the Christian would be more acutely conscious of his dependence upon God and less reliant upon his own accomplishments or abilities.

Whatever method or manner the Christian adopts to make his personal worship life richer, he ought constantly to keep in mind that his total life belongs to God. Living as a child of God can also be a life of constant worship. But the Christian must at all times be consciously aware that he must make expression of his love toward God in the way he performs the routine work of his calling. When he does this, then he has achieved an intimate union between worship and vocation.

Chapter 7

MONEY TALKS

FROM time to time pastors remind their congregations that we are living in an age of materialism. Most congregations accept this indictment rather placidly. After all, this is what preachers are expected to talk about. Very few people believe deep inside their hearts that they spend 90% of their time thinking about money. Their lives are so colored by the importance and necessity of money that they have a difficult time accepting the fact of its almost complete dominance of every phase of living.

Ben Hecht, noted scenario writer, may unconsciously reflect the fantastic mores of Hollywood when he writes: "Money-making is, if anything is, our national soul. It is the one thing on which all Americans think alike. At least I have met only a few extremely eccentric people who were not interested in making money. I have met a larger number who were tired of making it, but not tired enough to stop. . . . When most Americans read about the corruption and ruthlessness of the rich, they are inclined to grin. These malefactors are their dream

106

selves. The American does not aspire to overthrow the thieves and oppressors half as much as he does to become one of them."[1] There is too much truth in this assertion to condemn it as a sweeping generalization.

There are many other pieces of evidence which seem to indicate our preoccupation with money. When the news of President Eisenhower's heart attack saddened the nation and the world, what happened on Wall Street, that infallible barometer of American attitudes and aspirations? The newspapers headlined the biggest stock market collapse since October 1929. An anonymous New York Stock Exchange spokesman said: "The New York Stock Market merely reflects the hopes and aspirations, directly or indirectly, of every American, man, woman, and child."

One of the television sensations of 1955 was the spectacular rise of the program, "The $64,000 Question," that fabulous, utterly fantastic program which gave away small fortunes (even after income tax) to a variety of people. It was estimated that at the height of its popularity 80% of America's television sets were tuned in on the program. Millions watched breathlessly as the master of ceremonies tossed the questions at the victims. How do you explain this morbid interest in "The $64,000 Question"? Here is a comment by Robert Lewis Shayon in the *Saturday Review*: "This program, passing phenomenon as it may be, has struck so big a note precisely because it is an unconscious communal ritual. . . . Observe how they [the viewers] are dismembered by the trial, the suspense, the unendurable torment of

---

[1] *A Child of the Century* (New American Library), p. 414.

107

the hero who is expiating publicly their private, un-acknowledged *sin of greed.*" (Italics mine.)

Max Lerner, columnist for the New York *Post,* says that Louis G. Cowan, originator of the program, has come up with four ingredients which make "The $64,000 Question" popular. They are — and notice the order — (1) money; (2) information; (3) suspense; (4) documentary characters.

Paradoxically, even though the American may admit, grudgingly at times, his preoccupation with money, the majority will also confess that money cannot buy happiness, love, peace of mind. This is poignantly revealed by a young comic-strip artist, Stan Drake, in an interview with a reporter from *Editor and Publisher.* The reporter points out that the artist is young, handsome, owns three cars, has a sweet, attractive wife, two fine-looking sons, a modern home with private lake set in the rich beauty of Westport, Conn. The artist replied: "I make $85,000. That is, for the first time, I made that much last year. But I'm left with $30,000 after paying my three assistants, taxes, and expenses."

The reporter asked him: "But what's it like underneath? . . . What's the price you have to pay for the glory and the gold?"

Stan Drake replies: "It is a good life, a rich and successful one, but a lonely one, too. It's an unending grind, month after month. It's a trap I can't get out of. Yes, the income is first rate, but I often say to myself: 'So what! If I take time off, like today, I have to work night and day to catch up. What good does all the money do? There's little time to enjoy it.'" It's an old story, and its truth is admitted by even the thoughtless.

All too often the Christian is caught in the trap in

108

which Stan Drake and hosts of others find themselves. The Christian also feels that he will be judged by the price he has paid for his new car or by the size of the screen on his newest television set. If the adult Christian shrugs off these as a standard of judgment, he is painfully made aware of his inadequacies by his children, who are quick to point out that he does not provide as well as do the neighbors down the street.

MONEY

The attitude toward money can be wholesome and relevant to his faith once the Christian re-examines the conception of the Christian calling. What does it mean that we are called? Simply this: if we have been called effectively, we have accepted the Gospel. By accepting the Gospel, the announcement of God's love to man, the Christian puts aside his love of self — selfishness — and becomes preoccupied with his relationship to God and his neighbor.

Money is one aspect of life which the Christian can use to demonstrate the new status he has as the son or daughter of God. The way we use our money, the way in which we regard it, is a commentary on how we regard God's love toward us.

Thus money is not an end in itself but a means to realize a more complete expression of love which the Christian feels toward God. J. Pierpont Morgan is supposed to have complained in the early New Deal days about Franklin D. Roosevelt, "Roosevelt wants us all to have glass pockets." The Christian knows that his pockets are transparent at all times because he lives constantly under the eye of God.

The frightening aspect of money is that it can encourage the shoddy in us, or it can bring out the good and noble. Those green bills so handsomely engraved can serve as a trigger setting off a series of explosions whose effects can be either destroying or set up moral roadblocks. Our money affords us the opportunity to make a decision. For this opportunity we ought to be grateful, since there are not many areas left in life where we have freedom of choice.

We can decide to spend our money on cars, perfume, education, music, art, charity, drink. This is the challenging aspect of money. It has a potential not immediately discernible. It is a symbol of what we might be able to do.

At no other time has so much money been in the hands of so many people. The average annual income of the American ranges from $1,000 per individual to $4,000 per family. There does not seem to be statistical agreement here. Today there is a greater margin of this money left after the necessities of life have been paid for: shelter, clothing, food, taxes, security. But it is only money that is left over. The Christian has the power to translate the symbol into actuality.

The Christian recognizes also that "this money, like everything else we have in life, is not ours as an absolute right. It is one part of the goodness and bounty of God to us. We may have worked hard and earned it honestly, but all good things come ultimately from His hand, and we hold it in trust for Him. It is not our freehold, but leasehold, and we are exercising a stewardship over it in His Name. We have a certain freedom of choice about what we do with it, but the limits of that choice are set by Him, for we are answerable finally to Him for it." [2]

Someone has said that Jesus spoke more about money than any other subject. If this is so, it underlines the fact that God considers money one of the most significant criteria by which a man can be judged. A casual examination of both the Old and the New Testament indicates God's concern over man's attitude toward money. And yet all that money can possibly be is a means. Isolate yourself on a lonely Pacific island with several million dollars, and you will quickly discover the utter worthlessness of money in itself. Therefore the Christian must repeatedly remind himself that money is only a means. How he uses that means indicates his feeling of obligation to his calling.

RESPONSIBILITY

One of the common terms used in the church is *stewardship*.[3] Few people today appreciate this terminology because the only stewards they know may be dining car stewards, shop stewards in a factory, or airline stewardesses.

Instead of steward think of the word *manager*, specifically as this word relates to the management of a large corporation. Management has large responsibilities today, not the least being annual dividend return to the corporation's stockholders. Management does not own the company. There are instances where manage-

---

[2] John Murray, *The Daily Life of the Christian* (Philosophical Library), p. 87.

[3] According to the Oxford English Dictionary, *steward* may be traced to the two words *sty* and *warden*. A steward was originally the warden of the master's swine.

ment owns no stock in the corporation. However, management exercises every right of ownership: production, purchasing, investment, research, sales, advertising, labor relations. To all intents, management is the owner because of the functions it exercises. But no court would ever uphold the right of management to become owner, because the stockholders are absentee owners. Nor does management ever forget that once a year it must render a report to the owners on its conduct of the business.

✓ The Christian is also a manager. He manages his life, his property, his job, his health, his relationships with other people. He also manages his money. He may feel that this money is his own, the proper return on the labor he has expended to obtain it. Even such an assumption is mistaken. Second thought tells him that he did not even earn this money through his own efforts. He had to team up with other people, his neighbors, in order to earn this money. He did not manufacture that Chevrolet singlehandedly. The combined resources of thousands of people helped him to add a part of the manufacturing process to the car.

The thoughtful Christian realizes that ultimately he cannot even call his money his own. It comes to him because the crops were bountiful, the steel production was exceptionally high, the purchasing power of millions of people resulted in a certain amount of the money to be handed to him. If he wishes, he may pursue the progress of the money he has in his pocket to its first source: God the Creator. It is God who has given him the management of this money and it is to God that he is responsible for the disposition of that money. God expects competent management according to the several abilities with which He has endowed His managers.

What does God expect of His managers? He does not want waste, dishonesty, misuse of the money. God deplores miserliness. He does not want money hoarded in safety deposit boxes. He expects you to use His money in such a way that glory and honor is brought to Him through your use of that money in relationship to other people, your neighbors. He expects you to be conscious of this love you owe your neighbor. He asks that you spend that money in such a way as to convince God you are aware of your responsibilities to Him and those whom you are to love.

Recently 2,100 Chicago packinghouse workers walked sadly to the paymaster's window for their last checks. They lost their jobs. They were no longer needed, because the slaughtering and meat processing operations were moved elsewhere. The money doled out to the permanently dropped workers was severance pay. There would be no more money for the workers when this was spent.

"It's hurting to lose my job after 14 years," said Artter Harris, one of the discharged workers. "This is much more than losing my job. I've lost security as a family man . . . my insurance, my pension rights, hospitalization, seniority . . . my job."

A district director of the union to which these workers belonged said that finding new jobs for the workers is a problem because 70 per cent of them are over 40 years old.[4]

---

[4] The corporation remains nameless here. Readers interested in names and details may consult the Chicago *Daily News,* October 28, 1955. Lest the author be accused of bias against modern corporation practices, there are also many labor union practices which reveal a total lack of responsibility. Consult your newspaper.

The question of responsibility enters immediately, the responsibility of ownership and management to their neighbors who worked in the huge plant. Possibly the company was justified in closing its operations for the sake of efficiency. But are efficiency and profits more important than people?

All employers have the responsibility to see that no worker is sacrificed on the altar of profits and dividends. Labor unions have an equal responsibility to see that their members are not sacrificed for the sake of prestige and increased bargaining rights. Labor unions must render an accounting of their welfare funds to their membership at regular intervals.

Every Christian has a responsibility to support his family. This support is not an enforced duty, but it is an expression of the love which he in turn has received from God. Support of a family goes beyond the mere payment of taxes and the expenditure of sums of money for the necessities. This payment of money for the family requires also a wise knowledge of the special requirements of the various members of the family.

Extending beyond the immediate family environment, there is the financial responsibility a Christian feels toward the community. This expression of responsibility should find expression in the support of the various Community Chest endeavors, the special charitable drives undertaken locally, nationally, or internationally. But before sharing his money with these drives, he should become reasonably well acquainted with the objective of such endeavors.

Above and beyond the expenditure of money for others there is also the responsibility toward self. How to avoid the appearance of selfishness and the accusation of being a spendthrift is a difficult problem at times. There must be expenditure of money for care of the body, for the nourishment of the body, for shelter, and for all the other modern necessities. Perhaps in these areas of expenditures the Christian needs consecrated common sense and a constant knowledge of his or her own weaknesses. Nor should the Christian forget that he must first seek the kingdom of God. And he should remember the warning: "He that seeketh to save his life shall lose it."

Leo Tolstoy thought he had solved the troublesome problem of money and property by getting rid of everything and living again as a peasant. He was saluted as a great idealist, but no one heard the anguished cries of his family, which was forced to live in abject poverty because of a mental aberration in the father. In the process of living as a peasant, Tolstoy also neglected his own health and possibly hastened his own death. He had forgotten responsibility toward himself and in that process hurt others.

GOD AND MONEY

There is a specific agency through which the Christian can express his sense of love and obligation to God. That is the church, the company of the justified, the fellowship of saints. While it is readily granted that the organized church is frail and makes administrative mistakes which cause corporation executives to shudder, still it is the chief agency through which the Christian may share his money.

The demands of the church are endless. Crisis after crisis seems to arise, and as a result there are frantic appeals for more funds. No one disputes the urgency of the crisis nor the needs for money. The local congregation must support the ministry in its midst, provide an adequate structure for worship, be constantly alert to the educational needs of the membership, support the national body with which it has affiliated itself. Besides those local needs, there are area needs where groups of congregations may have erected a hospital, established a social welfare agency, participated in a number of chaplaincies to welfare or penal institutions. The national needs frequently overshadow the local requirements because an expanding population and increased enrollments at ministerial schools rise at a faster rate than the increase in local membership. Because the nation is not static in its development, general church bodies must meet the challenge of this continual growth. Frequently therefore the general body must issue appeals for more money to meet the situation of burgeoning national growth.

All this growth requires more money. No one pays for larger colleges, no one pays for more hospital chaplaincies, no one pays for the expansion of more mission congregations, no one except the individual Christian. The Christian pays the bills, and for generations to come he will have to pay the bills. He receives, and will continue to receive for the rest of his lifetime, appeals from his church to contribute generously to the needs of the church.

Now arises the tension in the life of the individual Christian. He readily acknowledges that God loves him. He is acutely aware of this divine grace in his own life. He feels that he owes God a tangible demonstration of love returned through the avenue of money he has earned. How much shall he give? If he buys a refrigerator for his home, has he shortchanged God? If his wife purchases a new coat for herself, has God lost out in the transaction? At what point does a Christian decide to do without some new plumbing fixtures in order that he might give to the drive for his church college's needed new dormitory? Shall he give proportionately of his income before deductions or only of his take-home pay? If he is a farmer, shall he give after he has deducted his operating expenses? Do you give of your gross or net income?

Many Christians feel that the answer is in the tithe, the ten per cent of their total income. There are two dangers in the tithe. The one danger is that the Christian is liable to have his giving become an automatic gesture. The other danger is that his giving of the tithe may create, unconsciously, within him a feeling of self-righteousness.

This is not to argue against those Christians who feel they must tithe. There have been countless testimonies to the effectiveness of the tithe in promoting spiritual growth. In its favor also is the argument of systematic giving. Most people are forgetful or lazy or prone to let the old Adam argue them out of regular giving.

The truth is that rules are difficult to state and, of course, to apply in the matter of handling one's money in relation to God. The most vital rule is the New Testament principle of giving as God has prospered. This places the Christian in the position of having constantly to restudy the blessings he receives from God. The motivating force in giving is always love, love toward God and His kingdom and your neighbor. When love is paramount in the handling of one's money, then there is less danger of becoming coldly calculating in how one's money is shared with God and neighbor. There may also be times when one gives impulsively out of a sudden burst of gratitude for blessings received. And there is no law against impulsive giving of this sort.

Chapter 8

NEIGHBORS AND COLORS

DURING his first year at Union Theological Seminary, James H. Robinson suffered a minor breakdown. Spending all his available spare time in study, often sleeping as little as three hours a night, he found his mind and body rebelling. When the seminary physician could find nothing wrong, he was sent to Presbyterian Hospital for observation. On the second day at the hospital, the specialist, who directed the interns and physicians in the examination, brought him into a lecture room and placed him, naked except for a loin cloth, on a little platform before the doctors, interns, and nurses.

The specialist had achieved a certain authority on the immunization of races to certain diseases and ailments. Now he lectured to the students at great length. Finally he said: "This boy's a Negro. You can see there's nothing physically wrong with him. His pain's imaginary. Let me explain further. This boy is ambitious beyond his capacity. Only a few generations removed from the jungles of Africa and slavery, he is unable to compete intellectually with men of the advanced white race."

The specialist paused a moment.

I will tell you what I would say to such a patient. I would say, young fellow, go back to the seminary, pack your things, get away from the real seat of your trouble. Our minds have great power over our bodies; otherwise you face a breakdown surely. There is no future for you in competing with men of the best cultural and mental heritage. Go down South, and get yourself a little church among your people. They need you, and there you can be somebody. None of you can hope to go beyond that level you yourself have attained.

When the young seminarian tried to reply, the doctor flung back at him, "I'm the doctor, you're the patient." [1]

When G. Elson Ruff wrote a spirited defense of the civil rights of Negroes in the pages of *The Lutheran,* he received this letter:

Sir:

If you uphold the Negroes like you pretend in that article, just get on any streetcar or bus and see how your pet Negroes act. If two or three are together, each takes a seat, and the white must sit next to them or stand. It seems to me the Lutheran churches got along very well for years without Negro members. The Negroes have churches of their own. Let them stay there.
                                    Emma Stumpp
                                    Chester, Pa. [2]

How does one explain these manifestations of prejudice, this unreasoning attitude toward people of another race or of another color? Gordon W. Allport, in his profoundly revealing study, *The Nature of Prejudice*

---

[1] *Road Without Turning: The Story of James H. Robinson, an Autobiography* (Farrar, Straus and Co.), p. 211.

[2] *The Lutheran,* August 25, 1948.

(Addison-Wesley), catalogs some of the reasons why people blindly adopt unreasoning attitudes.[3] There is the scapegoat theory; the frustration people feel when life turns the wrong way; aggression; guilt; projection. There are also the other theories which derive from psychoanalytic studies.

Whatever the explanations may be, the existence of prejudice, particularly among those who call themselves Christian, indicates a misconception on the part of the Christian of what his call, his new relationship to God, requires of him in expected behavior and thought.

ATTITUDES AND DOCTRINES

One of the great milestones in the long and painful history in America of achieving equality of opportunity for all races and colors is the May 17, 1954, U. S. Supreme Court decision outlawing segregation because of race or color in the nation's public schools. Chief Justice Warren delivered the court's decision which tossed out, so far as the schools are concerned, the doctrine of "separate but equal" facilities which had stood as the keystone of segregation laws since 1896. In the body of his opinion, Chief Justice Warren wrote that to separate children solely because of race generates feelings in their hearts and minds which may never be undone.

The loudest protests against the decision came from those states generally classified as belonging to the "Bible

---

[3] Another helpful analysis is Gerald W. Broomfield, *The Chosen People* (Longmans, Green). Dr. Broomfield offers a penetrating theological analysis of the attitude of the Dutch Reformed Church in the Union of South Africa. The troublesome *apartheid* theory and practice has the support of this most influential Christian body in South Africa.

Belt," where "fundamentalist Christianity" is proudly proclaimed. The Governor of Georgia said that this decision "raises a grave question as to the future of the nation." In Shellman, Ga., a Baptist minister who publicly expressed himself as being in favor of the Supreme Court ruling on segregation, was ousted from his church. The board of deacons demanded the resignation of the Rev. Henry A. Buchanan at a called church conference following Sunday school. The minister went to the church rolls, scratched out the names of himself and his wife, and wrote in the margin, "Cast Out," after the congregation voted 78 to 17 to accept the board's recommendation that the pastor be ousted.

Thoughtful Christians are, of course, disturbed because it required a legal decision to remind the churches they have failed, whereas secular, even anti-Christian agencies, have assumed the church's role. For the Christian knows that Holy Scripture does offer an outline of action which becomes an imperative to the sensitive conscience.

The first assumption every Christian makes — it is a basic article of belief — is that God created man. This is stated in Genesis. Beyond that descriptive statement of man's origin there is nothing about color or racial characteristics. There is also the statement that God was satisfied with His creation. Reading on through the various books of the Bible, we find no derogatory information about many of the Biblical characters in so far as skin coloration is concerned. The fabulous Queen of Sheba is generally supposed to have been of exceedingly dark pigmentation. Solomon rather liked her. The only racial group singled out for special blessings was the Israelite nation, not, however, because of its physical

122

characteristics but because God wanted it for a specific spiritual mission.

The New Testament bears eloquent testimony to the fact that neither the Lord Jesus Christ nor His Apostles discussed the matter of skin coloration. There was never any mention made of the importance of maintaining particular physical qualities. The primary emphasis was always on the fact that man, as a sinner confronting God, needed a Savior. Regeneration was the prime requisite. The quiet assumption is always that "God hath made of one blood all nations." Thus Simon of Cyrene, according to some legends, a black man, could bear the cross of the Savior without opprobrium from the chosen people. One of the points of the parable of the Good Samaritan is that a racial outcast administered mercy to one of the Lord's chosen.

Examination of the early church records and a study of great controversies of the church up to and including the Reformation reveal no evidence that St. Augustine, St. Jerome, St. Francis, Martin Luther, or any other great and near great man ever judged the worth of a person by the color of his or her skin.

Why are there Christians who are stubbornly opposed to admitting that people of darker hued skin have the same educational, religious, economic, and political rights? Some of this stubbornness may come from a misunderstanding of certain Bible passages, for example, Gen. 9:25. Here Noah pronounces a curse on his son Ham. "A servant of servants shall he be unto his brethren." Proponents of slavery and white superiority insisted that Ham was a Negro and that here God, speaking through Noah, set aside a special racial group.

They never explained how Noah, presumably a white man, could have a Negro son.

Another misuse of Scriptural passages to support the denial of basic rights to non-Caucasians is St. Paul's discussion of the matter of the giving of offense. In Romans 14 and in 1 Corinthians 10, St. Paul considers, among several items, the problem of offending the weaker brother. There is validity, naturally, in many situations "neither to eat flesh, nor to drink wine, nor anything whereby thy brother stumbleth, or is offended, or is made weak." But to use this and similar passages to keep in oppression a minority group, or to deny such a group blessings which a dominant racial group may already have, is a misunderstanding or perversion of Holy Scripture.

It is one of the strange perversities of human nature that men are always looking for a scapegoat. White Christians living where there are Negroes, Puerto Ricans, or Mexicans will almost unconsciously at times blame their unhappiness or misadventures on a minority group. At times the views of Christians take on the coloration of certain community patterns of thought. Frequently the Christian congregation finds itself defending respectability because the community expects respectability in a church.

Another reason Christians oppose racial integration or the frank acceptance of neighbors of colors other than white is that they, too, are subject to the same fears and the same repressions which afflict all people. The Christian is also subject to the feeling of job insecurity. The next time there is a dip in the economic index it is almost certain that the white Christians will be among those who raise the cry that Negroes have taken the jobs which rightfully belong to the whites.

Because Christians live in the economic and political climate of their community, it is not surprising to hear Christians expressing fears that property values decline when Negroes move into white neighborhoods. Reputable economists and the National Real Estate Board have shown this to be a totally unfounded notion. Nevertheless church boards in changing neighborhoods frequently argue that their church's property value will decline once Negroes move into the community. There may be some truth in the criticism frequently leveled at the churches by those unfriendly to the Gospel — that churches have erected property values as their god.

Christians and non-Christians alike fear minority groups because, in many instances, they have deep inside themselves hatreds and fears which they are unwilling to acknowledge. This is dramatically illustrated by the story of a young man, a DP, arrested by Chicago police for being a ringleader in the teen-age mobs persecuting the Negro family which had moved into the Trumbull Park area.

PERSECUTION VICTIM TURNS PERSECUTOR:
YOUNG DP SOBS STORY OF UNWITTING HATE

By Roy Topper

A youth confessing to a terrible hate tried tearfully to explain why he, who knew so well the lash of persecution, became a persecutor.

It was cruel and unreasonable hate that caused him to lead a bomb-and-brickbat campaign of racial terrorism on the South Side, said 18-year-old Imantis Pliuksis, 2319 S. Ridgeway.

"I knew what it was to be on the receiving end," he said. "I was born in Latvia. As a child I took it — first from the Nazis and then from the Russians."

Yet it was true, he said, as the state's attorney's office had charged, that he had been a ringleader of teen-age rioters who preyed on homes of Negroes in the Lawndale district.

Wanted Revenge

"It is the hate I had," he said. "It is the revenge I wanted — against someone, against anyone — for all the suffering of my people."

"I guess I picked on Negroes because everyone seemed to be picking on them," he said.

Pliuksis, an intense youth who speaks English fluently, brushed away tears frequently with the apology, "I am ashamed," as he analyzed his hate — and its consequences — in the lockup of the Marquette Police Station.

When he came to this country with his parents in 1949, he said, he discovered that even in this land of constitutional equality there were issues of racial hatred.

Attended High School

He came to feel this, he said, in his neighborhood associations and later at Harrison High School, which he attended for two years.

His own hate, he said, was imbedded deep beneath the scars of his family's European persecution. He first gave expression to it a year and a half ago, after an incident in Douglas Park.

"A bunch of boys demanded my money — I had only 18 cents," he said. "They took it, and they beat me up. Then I decided to get even."

He joined some friends, he said, "to deal with" reports that Negroes were preparing to move in their neighborhood.

"I learned to make bombs with 'hot fuses' on them," he said.

Then the gang, equipped for terror, began to seek out victims. It was indiscriminate choosing — any Negro family was fair game, he said.

Tells of Setting Fires

"We started to break windows and set fires. We began to throw out bombs," he related.

"My friends said it was the right thing to do. I convinced myself — maybe I was only pretending, though — that I was in something like the underground of Latvia and Germany."

He is scheduled to be heard Thursday in Boys' Court on charges of arson and exploding bombs in the city.

Now that he was in trouble, he said, he realized the futility as well as the injustice of his hate.

Chicago *Sun-Times*

WHEN RACIAL TENSIONS FLARE

What can a community do when racial tensions flare into riots? Are there agencies ready to offer constructive help? How can those who encourage violence be counteracted? How can the Christian churches and the men of good will anticipate and help prevent the madness of riots? The urgency of such questions, if not their answers, was thrown into dramatic focus by the tragic situation which developed in and near Trumbull Park Homes, a public housing project administered by the Chicago Housing Authority in an industrial area on Chicago's far South Side.

On July 30, 1953, Mr. and Mrs. Donald Howard and their two small children moved into an apartment in the 462-unit development. Not once in their six years of marriage had they had a home to themselves; they had lived with relatives, friends, even strangers. Donald

Howard is a native Chicagoan, a World War II veteran with service in the Philippines, a part-time postal employee. His wife, Betty, works as a telephone operator. When the family first applied for admission to the project last January, hopes for assignment seemed dim. Then, in May, Mrs. Howard heard that applications could be made directly at the Trumbull Park site. She did so, and on July 21 was informed that an apartment was available. She signed the lease, paid a month's rent.

The Howards are Negroes. The Chicago Housing Authority said later that it did not know this when Betty Howard applied at the management office; otherwise the ruling that the first admission of a non-white family to projects previously all-white must be approved by the agency's five-man commission would have applied. At that time, Trumbull Park Homes was one of only four projects among the twenty that the CHA operates which were not racially integrated.

On August 4 word spread that the Howards were Negroes, even though Mrs. Howard "looked white." That night a crowd of teen-agers gathered in front of the apartment. Bricks were thrown; one crashed through a window and landed inside. By August 6 the crowds had grown larger. Five more windows were broken. A gang of teen-agers tried to rush the apartment, but were stayed by a police detail. The next Sunday a crowd estimated at 2,000 gathered in the streets near by. Firecrackers were set off; jeering and yelling teen-agers roamed through the housing project. The city police department put into effect Emergency Plan No. 5.

On October 24 three other Negro families moved into Trumbull Park Homes. Mob violence increased, and 360 policemen were assigned to each of three daily eight-hour shifts. Some forty persons were arrested. In the weeks that have passed, special police have continued to patrol the area. The size of the round-the-clock details has been reduced, but the danger of violence has not lessened.

In permitting the other Negro families to move in, the CHA affirmed a nondiscrimination policy initiated some years ago. It has announced that applications for public housing from nonwhites are to be processed like any others, without referral to the commissioners. Meanwhile it is faced with a suit filed by the National Association for the Advancement of Colored People on behalf of thirteen Negroes previously denied admission to CHA projects. The suit insists that this denial violated state and federal laws guaranteeing equal rights in public housing.

The CHA was created 15 years ago as a municipal agency to develop and operate low-rent public housing. It has spent over $75 million for 10,000 units, which rent at around one fifth of a family's income — from $21 to $75. At the center of the present controversy is Elizabeth Wood, daughter of an Episcopalian lay missionary to Japan, who is the CHA's executive secretary. Despite catcalls from offended aldermen and excited real-estate operators, Miss Wood has kept politics out of the CHA. To many Chicagoans she has become a symbol of fair play and honest practice.

Chicago is in the midst of a vast program of throughway construction and public building projects involving expenditures of well over $1 billion. The CHA is clearing slum sites rapidly. In all this activity, some 20,000 Chicagoans are having to move from their homes. Eighty per cent of these displaced persons are Negroes — and

80 per cent of Chicago's Negroes are in the low-income group. The CHA has a backlog of 15,000 applications by Negroes for low-cost housing. Further complicating the situation is the fact that Negroes are coming to Chicago in increasing thousands, drawn by good job opportunities. Conservative estimates put their number in the city now at 650,000.

Who opposed the presence of Negroes in CHA developments? The list ranges from purely political opportunists and race haters to businessmen, surrounding residents, and those who say: "It's not the time; we must educate first." In the last category one often finds timid clergymen, labor leaders, and well-meaning civic leaders.

Alderman Emil V. Pacini, in whose 10th ward Trumbull Park Homes lies, is caught between conflicting interests. Shall he listen to the South Deering Improvement Association, which opposes the Howards' move-in, or shall he, as a Democrat, be loyal to Mayor Kennelly, who has backed the city's Commission on Human Rights and the use of the police emergency plan? Pacini insinuates that the CHA used "underhand methods" to move the Howards into the project; he is sure there was a plot somewhere to persuade them to settle in his ward. He has stated in a letter to a Chicago newspaper that the solution to Chicago's housing problem is to prevent the entry of "emigrants" from other states. However, he can cite no legal way in which this could be done.

Perhaps the most vociferous opponent of all efforts at racial integration in the area is Colonel Horace F. Wulf, who edits the *Daily Calumet,* a newspaper in an adjacent neighborhood. His paper has featured signed editorials, banner headlines, detailed news stories, and a "Blow Your Top" section, in which readers spell out their hatred of the Negro. Wulf, a reserve officer in the U. S. Army, was a combat officer in World War II. He is readily accessible to reporters and does not hesitate to state his views. Here is a sample of Colonel Wulf's editorial comment: "Some white areas may welcome other races with open arms. Bless them. But the folks of South Deering have not been sufficiently brainwashed to consent to such practice. Any race mixing must be done with a policeman's night stick. That will not work here." Asked why he campaigns so violently against the Howards, Colonel Wulf says: "I believe in the majority. That's the Constitution and that's American. . . . I'm 90 per cent realist and 10 per cent idealist."

The editor of the *Daily Calumet* prides himself on his regular attendance at different Sunday church services, which he features on Monday's front page with complete coverage of the minister's sermon. He himself is a member of a Methodist congregation in a neighboring community. If he is reminded that his devotion to church attendance and his antagonism toward the Howards are rather inconsistent, he replies: "The churches are only asking for trouble if they tell me who I've got to live with."

Another inciting influence is the White Circle League, headed by Joseph Beauharnais, who was convicted under a state group-libel law in 1952, a conviction later upheld by the U. S. Supreme Court. Beauharnais addresses disaffected groups, hoping to enlist 50 million people to uphold the "white man's rights" in the "racial war . . . declared upon (him) by the Negro." The White Circle League has distributed all over Chicago's South Side

131

incendiary leaflets pointing to the Trumbull Park Homes incident as proof of the need for the white race to unite to destroy the "malignant cancer of interracialism."

The absence of ready-made community organizations in the area which might lead in the formation of a sane approach to the situation contributed in the early months to the spread of antagonism and laid a foundation for violence.

There are no churches in the project itself. The failure of adjoining churches to provide either leadership or a courageous witness in the first months of trouble is a tragic commentary both on the timidity of the clergy and of church members. Here was an instance where personal ministry and lay witness could have helped in the easing of tension. Seemingly at the start the churches remained aloof from the Howard family itself. During the first troubled months no clergyman called on them.

Later on the Chicago Commission on Human Relations, the Chicago Council Against Discrimination, and the Chicago Lutheran Society for Better Human Relations began active educational campaigns.

What can be done in a situation of this kind? Trumbull Park Homes are in all parts of the United States and the world. In the first place, law and order must be maintained. The hoodlum element lies in wait for the slightest relaxation of police vigilance. This element as well as the upright citizenry will have to be convinced that Negroes and all minority groups are entitled to the exercise of the rights of citizenship.

The problem of overcrowding in the slums will have to be solved. Too often minority groups, migrating to urban centers, are forced to live in substandard housing. Adequate low-cost public housing must be erected. It must be demonstrated that Negro occupancy does not mean deterioration in property values.

Churches must remain in neighborhoods which are deteriorating. Altogether too many churches leave their physical property behind, migrate to the suburbs, and thus hope to avoid the problem of having undesirable people in church. In Chicago, fortunately, not all the inner city churches are leaving the blighted areas. An outstanding example is Warren Avenue Congregational Church on Chicago's West Side. This church attracts members from all racial groups. It exercises an aggressive leadership in a community where forty churches have died in recent years. Another is Salem Lutheran Church (Augustana Synod) on the South Side. Worship and Communion services are multiracial, and Negroes participate in all social groups — the women's federation, the men's brotherhood, the children's choir, the Boy Scouts.

The record of First Immanuel Lutheran Church (Missouri Synod) in the heart of a changing neighborhood offers a heartening example of a church refusing to be frightened by the influx of new people. Under the leadership of its courageous pastor and with the cooperation of a consecrated membership, First Immanuel today has people of all nationalities, races, and skin colors on the church rolls. An aggressive membership campaign seeks to gain more members for this church despite the racial origins of the prospective members.

More than two years have passed since the Howards moved into the Trumbull Park Homes. The Howards have since moved out of the project. But other Negro families are living among white neighbors. These Negro families must shop, travel to and from their jobs, play outdoors with the children — all under police surveillance. But they are staying. Not enough Chicagoans have learned that the Constitution guarantees the right to life, liberty, and the pursuit of happiness to all Americans regardless of the color of their skin.

BE CONSTRUCTIVE

There is a new atmosphere today. Ten years ago Westinghouse in its South Carolina plant would never have thought of putting Negroes and whites to work on the same semiskilled job. Today they work side by side. Walter Wheeler, president of Pitney-Bowes, says: "The head of the corporation has to lay down the policy (of integration) definitely and insist that it be carried out."

The church is reminding its membership of its duties in regard to minority groups. It is an unfortunate commentary that in the Roman Catholic Church an archbishop or a cardinal can issue an official pronouncement ending segregation practices in his parish. Generally, he can expect reasonable compliance after an initial period of misunderstanding or rebellion. Protestants do not operate by means of ukases issued by church dignitaries although there are times when the impatient feel this is the way to obtain immediate action.

Actually, to live in peace with one's neighbor regardless of the neighbor's racial background it is necessary for the Christian to realize in all his daily relationships that God's call to faith has no restrictive clauses. Nor does God make distinctions before the cross posted on Calvary. All are called to be kings and priests. There is no hierarchy of sainthood in heaven or on earth.

In order to drive this lesson into the heart so that it

is part of the daily beat of Christian action, proper attitudes must be developed in the home. Here is where the mother and father, exercising the right of their calling as Christian parents, may create the proper approach.

One mother was shocked to hear her third-grader say, "Niggers are dirty, mean people."

"Where did you hear that?"

"That's what they all say."

"Do you really think that's kind?"

"Well —"

In the days that followed she examined her own attitudes. She felt that there may have been times when derogatory references were made about minority groups. She recalled a heated conversation one evening with a neighbor across the backyard fence over the news that Negroes had moved into their community.

Because she was concerned over her child's unconscious reflection of a schoolyard attitude, she decided that in the home at least she would adopt a constructive attitude.

Operating on the basic assumption that God loves all people, she showed her third-grade son pictures of Negro scientists, educators, and artists. She played several phonograph records of Negro spirituals. She made a point of showing her child photographs in the picture magazines of noted accomplishments of Negroes. She and her husband would pointedly discuss a news item in the daily newspaper which referred to a praiseworthy action by a Negro. As time went on, these parents discussed other minority groups in their city: the Japanese, the Chinese, the Jews, the Mexicans. Always, however, the parents kept to the fore the central theme: God loves all people.

Sympathetic attitudes toward racial community problems can be fostered by the Christian in the various community organizations in which he may be active. One wise PTA member at a board meeting heard another board member express himself bitterly about a Negro family moving into the formerly all-white school district. Other board members expressed agreement or at least showed a vague discomfort. Rather than denounce or scold his associates, the wise board member said: "This is not a simple question. I appreciate your worries, but let's remember the U. S. Supreme Court has declared that Negroes have equal rights in education. Wouldn't it be interesting and instructive to devote one of our monthly programs to a discussion of the entire problem? Let's hear both sides. Isn't that the American way of doing things? Perhaps we can get three or four experts on a panel to lead the discussion."

The board members agreed rather reluctantly at first. Plans were made to have a panel discuss the various aspects of the changing racial picture in the school district. At the monthly PTA meeting a large crowd of interested parents and teachers was present. The three panel members discussed all aspects of the integration of minority racial groups into the neighborhood scene. When the time came for discussion, no inflammatory remarks were made, but there were many questions asked. Some of them were answered. The unanswered questions were written down, and the questioners were assured they would receive answers from experts.

Citizens of McPherson, Kans., faced a segregation problem which could have developed into an ugly situation had not the town's postmistress, Rozella Switzer, undertaken a one-woman crusade to educate her fellow citizens.

The story began when McPherson's Central College and McPherson College accepted a group of Nigerian students on missionary scholarships. One of the students, Elijah Odokara, a railway telegrapher who was taking a premedical course, came despite his grandfather's warning: "Christians don't practice what they preach."

One day when James Craig, a half-Scot Nigerian, went into a barbershop for his first American haircut, the barber refused to cut his hair. Augustine Njoku-Obu got a job in the local laundry and discovered he was being paid only half as much as the whites. The first time the boys went to the movies they were asked to sit in the balcony.

When Rozella Switzer was asked by McPherson College whether she could line up any warm winter clothes for the Nigerian students, she immediately invited the students to her home. She asked the students to tell her about Nigeria and their reactions to the United States. What she heard frightened her. "Discrimination makes me mad," Rozella Switzer said. "But this was different. This made me scared. All they knew about America was what they knew about McPherson. For the first time I really saw how important little things, a long way off, can be. We had to fight a one-town skirmish away out here in the middle of the United States."

She phoned the various merchants in McPherson, urging them to make contributions of winter clothing. They were bewildered by the request, but they responded when Rozella Switzer said: "All we have to do is to act like Christians." As time went on, she tried to help the people of McPherson understand why it was so necessary, both for their own self-respect and their nation's honor to be Christian and human in their treatment of these Nigerians.

She persuaded the barber to cut the boy's hair. The barber said sadly: "It hurt my business. Even some preachers told me I was doing the wrong thing." One minister warned Rozella Switzer: "We must be careful we're not called Communists." The local movie house permitted the boys to sit anywhere. The restaurant which had barred one of the boys from eating there now permits the Nigerians to eat with white diners.

McPherson, Kans., very likely is still a bit uncertain on just what attitude to take toward minority groups. The reaction of some is echoed by a letter writer who had read about Mrs. Switzer's efforts in *Time* and wrote indignantly: "Who in God's world cares to read of the misguided efforts of some obscure woman publicity seeker in Kansas?" It is certain, however, that the majority of McPherson's residents were challenged by the example of what one woman can do to get others to "act like Christians."

Perhaps the day is not too far distant when Elizabeth Montague Shimp's vision will be an actuality:

> I saw a miracle today:
> Two men from Georgia knelt to pray
> At Christ's Communion table.
> As brothers they approached the throne
> To cast their common burdens down;
> And round them shone a holy light —
> For one was black, the other white.[4]

---

[4] Reprinted by permission of the *Christian Century* and the author.

Chapter 9

TWENTY-FOUR HOURS

"God is the inexplicable whole of existence."
                                    SOREN KIERKEGAARD

THE Christian is an instrument. He has "put on Christ" in Baptism. He is a living member of Christ's body. This body is the church. Christ acts through the Christian. He is the Head, the Christians constitute the body. The head asks the body to perform tasks, to carry out wishes and commands. Once an individual has "put on Christ" his life is dedicated entirely to God. His life is no longer his own. He lives in a holy and intimate relationship with Christ.

As aware as the Christian is of this incomparably glorious calling, he is also aware of the tensions which arise daily. The Christian must make decisions involving good and bad choices. On the one hand he finds himself deciding in favor of that which, according to his point of view at the moment, is excellent but contrary to divine standards. When the Christian does that which is good, he is haunted by the knowledge that he might have done better. His successes too often seem trivial triumphs in the blinding glory of God.

The Christian must frequently make technical decisions. The farmer must decide which chemicals are to be added to the soil. The engineer may have to make a technical decision which suddenly involves him in an ethical or moral dilemma.

As the hours of the day roll on the Christian becomes increasingly aware of the difficulties he faces in leading a consistent life as a member of the body of Christ. He discovers that the Christian life can involve him in complexities which are both disturbing and upsetting. Sometimes there will be those who despair. When the contradictions beset them too fiercely, they feel it would be the better part of discretion to abandon all faith. Of course, it should be pointed out that there are not too many such sensitive Christians.

Every Christian feels at some time or other the impermanence of the work he does. The dishes washed in the morning must be washed again after the evening meal. The road builder knows that his carefully engineered highway will someday be torn up and redesigned. The newspaper editor knows that this day's newspaper wraps up the next day's garbage. The actor's performance may enthrall thousands for a few glittering hours, but his work will be but a faintly lingering memory after a few weeks.

Each day has its small and large crosses. The small cross may be the nagging knowledge of work never quite done, or of disagreeable associates in office or factory, or stubborn material, or an insoluble problem. The large cross may be the heartache of unfulfilled honorable ambition, the sorrow which comes from working for an ungrateful or unappreciative employer.

These crosses are not to be carried alone, nor are they to be considered irritations. Let each cross serve as a reminder of the cross carried by the Lord Christ through the streets of Jerusalem to Calvary. These crosses, carried in faith, are hallowed. They are to serve as blessed reminders of the great redemptive work of Christ. Each cross, each burden of the day, can serve as another thread which intertwines the Christian with his fellow Christians; for all Christians have their individual crosses to carry in pain and sorrow. These crosses are common bonds of fellowship in the communion of saints.

Every Christian ought to practice the daily discipline of subduing the flesh, that rebellious part of him which is in constant revolt against God. Dietrich Bonhoeffer, the martyred Lutheran pastor, shortly before his execution by the Nazis, said: "The real difference in the believer, who follows Christ and has mortified his will and died after the old man in Christ, is that he is more clearly aware than other men of the rebelliousness and perennial pride of the flesh; he is conscious of his sloth and self-indulgence and knows that his arrogance must be eradicated. Hence there is need for daily self-discipline." [1]

Is there any prescription for the Christian who wishes to become firmer in his calling? What sort of procedure can he observe through the allotted twenty-four hours which we call day and night?

---

[1] In his book, *The Cost of Discipleship* (New York: Macmillan), p. 146.

141

1. Begin the day with prayer: a conscious spoken word of praise and thanksgiving and a petition for grace and strength throughout the day.

2. Attempt to do at least one conscious act of kindness which is motivated only by Christ's love. This act may be a word or a deed.

3. On the basis of some news item, either heard or read, consider the working of God. How was God manifested in this particular happening?

4. Through some word or action make a conscious witness to Jesus Christ. This may be related to Point 2.

5. Ask yourself: In what way during the hours of this day have I been aware of my calling in Christ?

6. Close the day with a conscious and deliberate communion with God through His Word. Ask forgiveness for the day's sins, and pray for blessings during the passage of the night hours.

The Christian ought to learn to enjoy God's world. There are so many earnest Christians who are blind to the beauties of the mountains and plains. They are deaf to the harmonies of a Mozart or Beethoven. They fail to catch the rhythms of the great poetry of past and present. They refuse to be enriched and exalted by the tragedies of the world's great playwrights. They cannot see the incomparable glory of a Rembrandt self-portrait or a Cezanne still life. They plod through life, blinkered on the right and left. They fear to smile and laugh. They wonder if it is proper to relax. Small wonder that sometimes Christians succumb to mental or spiritual aberrations. They have not learned the joy of relaxation through sports, hobbies, art, music, movies, great creative writing.

The Christian is a whole man. For him God created the world. For him God maintains the world in its orderly working. For him God is to be found everywhere.

In *The Upper Room* Lydia E. Gruchy tells the story of an old stone church on the Island of Jersey in the English Channel. The church has withstood the ravages of time even though much of the cliff on which it was built has been worn away by the water and storms of the passing centuries.

"The walls of the church are made of stones of all sizes, for every member of the congregation contributed to them at least one stone, the best he could carry. The master builder used them all. There they are to this day. The rocks brought by the men have their place in the foundation. Stones large and small are there, and even pebbles that mothers had placed in the tiny hands of the babies."

Isn't this a symbol of the Christian in his vocation or calling? We are all workers. We bring our daily labor, the significant and the trivial, to the total task of living. We are building the structure of God's world. We are workers with Him.

No task of the day's hours can, therefore, be unimportant. The Christian has been called to build. This is the knowledge which sustains him in his vocation. This is his motive for living.

HELPFUL BOOKS

If this book has stimulated your interest in Christian vocation, further reading in the following books will offer you additional insights. The starred books may prove a trifle ponderous for the reader not theologically trained. Nevertheless, if you are willing to devote the extra mental effort to such reading, you will be amply rewarded for the time and thought you spent on these books.

The Daily Life of the Christian. By John Murray. Philosophical Library

Your Other Vocation. By Elton Trueblood. Harper

Ethics in a Business Society. By Marquis W. Childs and Douglass Cater. Mentor

Christian Faith and My Job. By Alexander Miller. Association Press

Here I Stand. By Roland Bainton. New American Library

Adventures in Politics. By Richard L. Neuberger. Oxford

The Christian World Mission in Our Day. By K. S. Latourette. Harper

The Cost of Discipleship. By Dietrich Bonhoeffer. Macmillan

Conscience and Compromise. By Edward L. Long, Jr. Westminster

The Belief in Progress. By John Baillie. Scribner's

Day by Day We Magnify Thee. By Martin Luther. Muhlenberg

The Quest for Holiness. By Adolf Koeberle. Augsburg

The Household of Faith. By T. Ralph Morton. Iona Community

Moral Man and Immoral Society. By Reinhold Niebuhr. Scribner's

The Church and Contemporary Change. By G. Bromley Oxnam. Macmillan

° *The Righteousness of God.* By Gordon Rupp. Philosophical Library

Christianity and Civilization. By Emil Brunner. Scribner's

Work and Vocation. Ed. by John Oliver Nelson. Harper

Let God Be God. By Philip S. Watson. Muhlenberg

Guide to Christian Living. By Otto W. Heick. Muhlenberg

Careers for You. By Erma Paul Ferrari. Abingdon

Doing the Truth. By James A. Pike. Doubleday

* *Faith Active in Love.* By George W. Forrell. American Press

Careers for Christian Young People. By Margaret Graham. Van Kampen

Our Calling. By Einar Billing. Augustana Book Concern

* *Christian Vocation.* By W. R. Forrester. Scribner's

Great Voices of the Reformation, ed. H. E. Fosdick. Modern Library

The Lonely Crowd. By David Riesman. Doubleday

Every Occupation a Christian Calling. By John Oliver Nelson. Association

Renewal of Faith. By Alexander Miller. Doubleday

Three Treatises. By Martin Luther. Muhlenberg

* *Ethics of Decision.* By George W. Forrell. Muhlenberg

The Lutheran Reformation. By Jerald C. Brauer and Jaroslav Pelikan. Student Service Commission

Modern creative literature abounds with excellent novels, plays, and poetry which deal with the theme of Christian vocation both from a positive and a negative point of view. The outstanding play of our generation which shows the futility of an existence based on materialism is Arthur Miller's *Death of a Salesman.* Among the novels, the following, published within the past decade, will offer interesting insights into various aspects of vocation:

Guard of Honor. By James Gould Cozzens. Harcourt, Brace

Executive Suite. By Cameron Hawley. Doubleday

The Dollmaker. By Harriette Arnow. Viking

Round the Bend. By Nevil Shute. William Morrow

Sincerely, Willis Wayde. By John P. Marquand. Little, Brown

The Carmelite. By Elgin Groseclose. Macmillan